Beyond
the Fear
of Death

E. G. Sherman Jr., PhD., D.S.T., D.A.

ISBN
979-8-88945-144-0 (Paperback)
979-8-88945-145-7 (eBook)

Brilliant Books Literary
137 Forest Park Lane Thomasville
North Carolina 27360 USA

TABLE OF CONTENTS

DEDICATION

This book is dedicated to my parents, the late Eugene Sherman, Sr., and Mary Martin Sherman, who were the first teachers in teaching my siblings—the late Willie Frank and James Lord—Larry Wendell, Mary Eunice, and Glory Nadine—to learn the childhood prayer. It was "now lay me down to sleep, I pray the Lord my soul to keep; if I should die before I wake, I pray the Lord my soul to take." As we grew older, they introduced us to the Lord's Prayer as recorded in Matthew 6:9–12. They later taught us to individualize our prayers. Dad and Mom always had a period of prayer before each of our daily family meals, then known as breakfast, dinner, and supper. Our early exposure to prayer continued in both the school and church settings.

The book is also dedicated to the countless persons for whom I have prayed within my ministry as pastor, teacher, counselor, at marriage ceremonies, in domestic crises, during family adversities, in hospital confinement at nursing homes, funerals, and crises in living.

Lastly, this book is dedicated to all who have chosen to read it and, hopefully, will gain confidence in the value of prayer in coping with the reality of daily living and preparing for the eternal transition when "ye shall be no more." Such was the case of my beloved wife of thirty-nine years, Dr. Dolores E. Sherman, who underwent this inevitable transition on December 12, 2008.

PREFACE

Death is universal! Death is unavoidable! Death is final! Death—for some—is welcomed! But death for many is feared. Yet humanity has encountered death since the beginning of time. This fact is disclosed in both biblical and secular histories. The first biblical family—Adam, Eve, Cain, and Abel—faced death when Cain killed Abel, his brother. Ancient Egypt, often referred to as the cradle of civilization, held elaborate services for their Pharaohs and entombed them with precious artifacts in elaborate burial containers. It was also in Egypt that the art of embalming was instituted.

Since the beginning of civilization, whether viewed against biblical or secular history, humankind has had to confront death. Varied have and continue to be reactions to both dying and death. Hence, there seems to exist a need of pragmatic information on the reality of dying and death. Accordingly, this book is a philosophical study of the inevitable fate that awaits the whole of humanity, the fear engendered by thoughts of dying and some practical suggestions for living without being besieged by a recurring feat of death.

This book, *Beyond the Fear of Death*, was prepared in response to the many calls (pastor, teacher, gerontologist) with questions about death, dying, and a life after death. After considering those concerns, I decided to write this book titled *Beyond the Fear of Death*. Hopefully, it will provide some comfort to the readers.

ACKNOWLEDGMENT

This book is dedicated to the numerous students who enrolled in my class, death and dying, at Albany State University, Albany, Georgia, the students in my weekend seminary class at the Albany Center of Bethany Divinity College and Seminary, Dothan, Alabama, those trainees in my seminars on this topic, members of Institutional First Baptist Church, Albany, Georgia, where I serve as a pastor and have delivered eulogies, and to my late wife of thirty-nine years, who underwent the final transition on December 15, 2018 and whose eulogy I delivered.

INTRODUCTION

This study grew out of the author's dual experiences as a Professor of Sociology at Albany State University, Albany, Georgia for thirty-five years, a founding pastor of Institutional First Baptist Church in the same city, and weekend Dean of a Theological Center from Bethany Divinity College and Seminary in Dothan, Alabama (1988–2011).

These two professions—sociology and theology—have provided a laboratory opportunity to discern the fear of death in the secular and in religious contexts and, concurrently, study this fear from a theoretical and academic orientation. Within both settings, the author has found that people react in various ways to the thought of death. Among the more frequent responses are denial, anxiety, fear, and anticipatory grief. However, the most frequently expressed attitude has been the fear of death.

Since the fear of death is so widespread and, yet, all mortals must die, this book was planned to offer an approach to aid in the development of a realistic attitude toward death. Hopefully, it will contribute to the perceptual growth necessary to attain an attitude of confidence and trust in the ultimate source that undergirds life, and concurrently, it will contribute to a consciousness that is beyond the fear of death.

SOME PARAMETERS OF THE BOOK

Emergence of the Death Education Movement

Death related topics are widespread in academic, medical, theological, legal, and increasingly, in the laity. Existing research documents the fact that death is a topic that causes varied reactions among people. One of the most pervasive reactions is that of fear; it is found in the laity but also in a segment of the professional arena and the collegiate student body. This writer, a sociologist, theologian, and philosopher, taught a course titled *Death and Dying* at the university level for more than two decades. That course always closed during preregistration. The enrollees included employees and professional in the helping services.

In addition to the regular students at the university, the hospice volunteers were required to complete a core on death and dying with the training being taught within the hospice facility. Another academic thrust was to offer a core on death and dying for students who were in training to become volunteer chaplains at the local hospital; the program was conducted in an accredited Chaplaincy setting.

Lay persons are also showing an interest in death education. Increasingly, they are reading inspirational and/or academic sources and frequently enrolling in death related workshops, seminars, and continuing education courses.

Pioneer Publication on and Governmental Interest in Death

Although interest in death as a focus of academic study was a product of the '70s, there had been sundry references to, dialogues regarding, lectures on, and writings about it long before the National White Conference on Aging in 1961. In fact, Herman Feifel published a book in 1959 entitled, *The Meaning of Death*. Since that time, a plethora of articles, books, and essays have been released on the topic of death and dying.

Beginning of the Hospice Movement

In addition to the academic dimension of death, there occurred a pragmatic orientation designed to offer palliative care of terminally ill cancer patients. The program was founded in England by Cicely Saunders who designated it as hospice. That hospice movement soon spread to America, first in the New England (Yale) and later throughout the nation. Congress recognized the value of this initiative, and therefore, it added Medicare coverage for persons so afflicted (1982).

The contemporary hospice program has been expanded to include noncancer patients but with a terminal condition. The program now follows one of two general models: Not for profit and for profit. They tend to follow one of their modalities: An existing medical facility, a freestanding unit, and part of a long-term care facility.

The academic development of death and dying (thanatology), a concept derived from the Greek God of death, Thanatos, experienced rapid and systematic academic growth during the '70s. A partial listing of authorities, without any attempts to evaluate the sources, is listed below. The focus instead is to provide interested persons with a few sources to aid in their reading and possible research. Included are:

- Herman Feifel, *The Meaning of Death*
- Elizabeth Kubler Ross, *On Death and Dying*

- Jessica Mitford, *The American Way of Death*
- Leming and Dickinson, *Understanding Dying & Bereavement* (*The text used in my course on Death and Dying-An extensive list of references on this topic can be found in texts on the subject, journals, and the web search.*)

Gauging the Fear of Death

Although it is generally assumed that some people, especially Americans, have a fear of death, it is untenable to conclude that the fear can be collapsed into a single and inflexible form. Accordingly, it is herein submitted that the attitude toward death can be fitted into a categorical scale consisting of four distinct reactions that include:

1. *Fear of death.* This is the most emotional response to the idea of death; it is rooted in worry about the type, experience, time, and consequence of death.
2. *Denial of death.* Reaction at this level consists largely of not allowing the mind to focus on death.
3. *Anxiety regarding death.* A state of lingering awareness that death is inevitable and an ever-present concern about its nature and timing.
4. *Acceptance of death.* A realistic acknowledgement that death is inevitable and, concurrently, efforts to minimize thoughts of it.

The Place of Death. From Colonial times to about the 1950s, most deaths occurred at home. After the close of World War II, the advances in medical technologies along with the expansions in hospital services, there occurred a shift in locus of death from the home to the hospital. This trend was accentuated with the Enactment of Medicare and Medicaid. Hence, there was an increase in the number of non-home deaths. This trend was further accentuated with the expansion of the hospice movement. The hospice services encompassed four options, namely: Hospice within the context of a hospital, a free-standing hospice program, hospice within an extended care facility, and hospice within the patient's residence.

Body Disposal. The reality of death necessitates the need for a socially approved method for disposing the body of the descendant. Initially, it must be determined if the person was an organ and/or body donor. Next will follow the preparation of the body for burial or cremation. Increasing, this latter method is becoming more frequent, owing to cost and decreasing stigma against it.

Post Death Activities. The occurrence of death is ultimately followed with an extensive set of activities that included, but not limited to: Body removal and disposal, fulfilling of financial obligations, probating of estate, and the process of adjusting to forever living without the physical presence of the descendant.

Some Techniques for Coping with the Fear of Death. Since it is now known that human behavior is non-instinctive and is rather shaped by behaviorism (learning), it follows those thoughts, views, and beliefs acquired over an extended period of time. Fear, in this connection, is acquired through human interaction and/or personal experiences. Although, the notion may seem real to the individual, even to a level where it generates emotional and behavior responses, this book's present theoretical, theological, and practical methods to cope with, if not eliminate, the fear of death.

Epilogue or Postscript. Life is a mere transitory sojourn between birth and death. It starts with efforts to activate the breezing process and ends when technological efforts fail to continue the respiratory activities. Hence, the ultimate conquer claims the individual. While this ultimately reality is widely known, there yet exists the attitude of fear within a segment of the human population. This mindset is acquired rather than biological in nature, and it can, be diminished—if not eliminated. Numerous are the techniques including psychotherapy, pastoral counseling, group therapy, and reading on the topic of ear in general. This book is intended as a resource designed to quell if not eliminate the fear of death.

The author has interspersed this book with copies of workshops and/or seminars that he conducted. Hopefully, this inclusion will acquire both a greater interest in and appreciation in gerontology and death and dying—an inevitable destiny that awaits humanity (Ecclesiastes 3:2).

CHAPTER 1

WHAT IS FEAR?

As a general proposition it can be stated that mankind, under most circumstances, prefers life to death. This view is consistent with Wolfe's assertion that "Man loves life and loving life, he hates death." Accordingly, humankind seeks to prolong its earthly sojourn—efforts to attain the goal of longevity include medical checkups, dieting, rigorous programs of exercise, and many other preventive activities. Yet every individual eventually dies not because of neglecting but owing to the fact of being mortal.

The human group has a multiplicity of personifications about death. Probably, the more frequently used term is the grim reaper. However other designations include: The pale rider, the ever-present foe, the great equalizer, and the final visitor. Opposing ideas include: The benevolent friend, the eternal companion, and the guardian angel.

Death transcends all forms of social differentiation; it seems to come sooner and more frequently improvised areas than in the affluent sector of society. However, death will occur in all groups and eventually for every moral being. Hence, death is the final conqueror for the whole of humanity.

Death means to be absent, to be freed from the body, to be alone, to be at rest, to be forgotten, and to have another and final status, deceased. It is largely owing to these characteristics, along with the uncertainty of how and when death will occur, that causes *the fear of death*. To provide a practical approach for becoming more informed on dimensions of dying and death, this book, *Beyond the Fear of Death*, has been prepared.

And even speculation have occurred in the discipline of psychology William McDougall, an early psychologist posited the notion that human behavior was largely controlled by instincts which were part of human nature. His views were later modified, and some rejected, as Psychology became more formalized. Using the McDougall postulate, fear would be a part of human nature. Hence, every would have the potential to manifest fear when confronted by certain situations. This potentiality was an expression of an instinct. This word, as defined on Foxfire, is "an inborn pattern of behavior that is characteristic of a species and is often a response to specific environmental stimuli: the spawning instincts of salmons."

The pioneer psychoanalysis, Freud, included instincts as part of human nature. He taught that humanity is constantly struggling between two instincts, one for life (Eros) and the other for death (Thanatos). Accepting the tenability of this Freudian theory, it follows that fear may well be a concern for those who cling to Eros. It must be noted, however, that Freud's contributions to psychology and psychoanalysis were numerous, but his three-stage development of personality that is most frequently cited; they are the id, ego, and superego.

The field of psychology emphasizes more on behavioral rather than the instinct theory of human behavior. Within that context, emphasis is placed on nature and not nature. Thus, attitudes, actions, and beliefs are all acquired after birth, including fears. The psychologists do recognize the roles of some physiological actions such as the blinking of the eyes and the feeling of hunger at the sight of food. But the scholars refuse to classify those responses as instincts. They emphasize rather a phenomenon known as classical conditioning. Essentially, that theory postulates a twofold dimension of an action; first, an action that is rewarded leads to reinforcement while, secondly, one that causes punishment tends to be discontinued. This principle is often referred to as reward vs. punishment. While this principle may have widespread implications in inducing desired behavior, it is difficult—if not ineffective—in eradicating the fear of death.

The fear of death in humankind is also a topic in the social sciences, particularly sociology. Therein it is taught that the biological baby must undergo a series of continuous human contacts; these experiences are known as socialization. Initially, these interactions occur within a family setting known as the primary group, a term coined by Charles Horton Coley. He described the family as primary in size, characterized by a "we are feeling," cooperation, and empathy. Within that network of human contacts, the infant acquires some knowledge based through instruction and imitation of those within its environment. The acquired information includes name, family members, other relatives, dos and don'ts, aspirations, traditions, and yes, superstitions and fears. It is an unfortunate fact conversations and actions involving death are often acquired by listening and observing actions of adults as they respond to the reality of death. Hence, if the adults convey fear there is a probability that the child will acquire a similar attitude. The topic of death is referenced in the Bible (KJV). Therein, is presented as an inevitability occurrence: Deuteronomy 34:5, Job 14: 1, Psalm 23:4, (Psalm 90: 10, Ecclesiastes 3:2, Luke 16:22, Matthew 24:42, 2 Peter 3:9, and Revelation 20:4–6; 12–15. While these and many other Scriptures embody teachings on the finality of death, the Bible also is replete with references to coping with the fear of death. Two Old Testament Scriptures that address this topic are: Job 19:25 where he asserted, "For I know that my redeemer liveth, and that he shall stand at the latter day upon this earth. And though after my skin worm destroy this body, yet in my flesh shall I see God." As noted in Job's articulation, he had no fear of death, nor did he seek its avoidance; he rather acknowledged its forthcoming reality. He, therefore, developed a twofold view of life and its aftermath. Accordingly, he recognized the human inability to avoid death and he, therefore, looked forward to the ultimate return of God at the time he (Job) would see and be in the presence of God.

The second scriptural approach for coping with the fear of death is David's confidence as found in the Psalm 23. In that writing is found David's view of death, it is encoded in the words, "Ye, though I walk through the valley of the shadow of death, I will fear no evil; for thou art with me; thy rod and thy staff they comfort me."

As noted, both Job and David were aware of the certainty of death, but neither expresses any fear regarding its eventuality. That confident attitude toward death was also evident in the life of some New Testament personalities, two of whom are Jesus and Paul. Jesus, the Son of God (Matthew 3:17, John 3:16) was keenly aware of both his earthly mission and subsequent death. Yet he continued his ministry that ended with the crucifixion where he, amidst the agonizing pain remained coherent and uttered, "Father, into thy hands, I commend my spirit" (Luke 23:46). The great persecutor of the early church, Saint Paul, who became an ardent defender of the young Christian Church, made nonfear statements about the reality of death. On one occasion, he referred to death as being absent from the body and present with the Lord (2 Corinthians 5:8). Later as he recognized the forthcoming end of his life, Paul wrote, "For I am now ready to be offered, and the time of my departure is at hand. I have fought a good fight, I have finished my course, I have kept the faith" (2 Timothy 4:6–7).

The topic of attitudes and reactions to death is found in music, dramas, sermons, tributes, literature, and politics. Probably, the most well-known and frequently cited one is found in William

Cullen Bryant's Thanatopsis, a concept that denotes a view of death.

> *So live, that when thy summons comes to join*
> *The innumerable caravan which moves*
> *To that mysterious realm where each shall take*
> *His chamber in the silent halls of death,*
> *Thou go not,_like the quarry-slave at night,*
> *Scourged by his dungeon; but, sustained and soothed*
> *By an unfaltering trust, approach thy grave,*
> *Like one who wraps the drapery of his couch*
> *About him, and lies down to pleasant dreams.*

Reference to fear was echoed in a political speech delivered by Franklin D. Roosevelt as he sought to calm and motivate the nation during the Depression of the 1930s. He said, "The only thing we have to fear is fear itself (Foxfire).

While fear of death is probably the most pervasive type, it nonetheless exists in other areas of human life. There are, for example, biological fears that include failing health, damaging accidents, increasing dependency, alternative living arrangements, and expiring in a nursing home. Fear in areas of continuing psychological normality is another concern during the sojourn of life. Many are the psychological malfunctions that engender fear, but Alzheimer's disease is the most dreaded one. A third area that causes fear is within the social arena. In contemporary times, people are bombarded with numerous fear-producing situations. These include home invasion, assault, robbery, rape, stroke, released from employment, and becoming homeless. The fourth area of fear is in the religious arena. It can be viewed on two different levels, the first of which is fear regarding the ultimate outcome after death, i.e., heaven or hell (the Christian perspective).

Next is the fear of death as reflected in the life of biblical personalities. In the Old Testament is found the account of Moses seeking to avoid returning to Egypt because he had earlier killed an Egyptian. Next is the account of Elijah fleeing from Jezebel after having defeated Baal. From a slightly different perspective, the New Testament depicts fear during the ministry of Jesus. In one situation the Master is recorded as having said unto his followers, "Fear not little flock for it is your father's good pleasure to give you the kingdom" (Luke 12:22). The next selected reference is found in Revelation 2:10, where Jesus said, "Fear none of those things which thou shalt suffer."

While the range and types of fear exceed the intent of this book, it is herein asserted that the fear of death—whether openly acknowledged or concealed—is a reality for many individuals. It may exist as a mere attitude. It may be reflected in a behavior pattern, or it may be a topic of avoidance in conversations.

Owing to the varying intensity that can undergird the fear of death and the nonclinical foundation of this book, no attempts are made to offer or recommend therapies. It is submitted, however, that this fear of death—when diminished or eradicated—will provide relief from a lingering thought and give way to a new unpredictable; and its expiration process is a variable.

The mode for determining death has evolved from an in-home type (Colonial times to the 20th Century) to the medical model in the contemporary era. In the so-called home mode, a mirror was placed over the dying person's noise to gauge whether there were any signs of breezing. Should no vapor appear on the mirror, the patient was determined to expired. A second method was to place one's ear over the person's chest to determine if there were yet signs of a heartbeat. Another in home method was to feel the pulse to detect if the individual was yet alive. Collectively, these three methods were nonmedical means to determine if the cardio-pulmonary had ended, thereby warranting the conclusion that the person was dead.

CHAPTER 2

WHAT IS DEATH?

This chapter, "What Is Death," creates inquires, regrets, preparation, avoidance of discussion, restless nights, and an ultimate decision to commence planning for the reality, and "mending of broken relationships."

Death, by definition and reality, is the permanent separation of all signs of life from the human body. I recall a definition in a book I used for my course in *Death and Dying* where Leon Kass (1971, pg. 69), defines death simply as "the transformation from the state of being alive to the state of being dead." Admittedly, numeral definitions have since been added to this definition. Also, humor, poetic statements, and biblical assertions have been included, two of which are: "Doctor, doctor, will I die?" The doctor replied, "Yes, my child, and so will I." The second response is found in the Bible—A time to be born and a time to die (Ecclesiastes).

This topic of death is often avoided, deliberately distorted, and even terminated by the host. But it is a destiny that awaits every alive mortal. Hence, people are alive or dead, unless some may choose to hasten death by suicide.

In my class on *Death and Dying*, I came across several references on death. The two most frequently cited were *What Is Death* and *The Fear of Death* (R. Leming). Owing to the recurring about the *Fear of Death*, I approved to include *Content of Death Fear* in this manuscript. Leming wrote eight types of death fears that can be applied to the death of self and the death of others:

1. Dependence
2. The pain in the dying process
3. The indignity in the dying process
4. The isolation, separation, and rejection that can be part of the dying process
5. Leaving loved ones
6. Afterlife concerns
7. The finality of death
8. <u>The fate of the body</u>

As a pastor, emeritus professor, member of Hospice Committee, eulogist, writer, and widow (2008), I know the grief of countless persons—including loss of two brothers, eulogist for my father, mother, an aunt and her husband, a cousin and her husband, and many of my church members. In the meantime, Covid-19 has been and is increasing its grip on humanity (note number 4).

In the meantime, *Death and Dying* authorities with numerous scholars have submitted categorical theories of death. In understanding *Dying, Death, and Bereavement* by Leming and Dickinson, those scholars submitted several approaches to the study of dying and death (pp. 17–27), namely: The biological approach, the psychological approach, the anthropological approach, the sociological approach. No interpretation nor evaluation of these approaches are herein included. However, interested readers are referred the earlier cited references.

Although there are many writers, newscasters, preachers, street salespeople, and other word-of-mouth sales, this writer merely focuses on the dissemination of factual information. Using his academic, theological, and practical experiences, he will cite some theological (sermons) to help the reader cope with and hopefully, rise beyond the fear of death.

Since it is a fact that every born person will die. The Bible, Revelation 14:13 asserts, "Blessed are those who die in the Lord." Recognizing this reality, I am submitting this sermon entitled, *The Blessed Dead*. Hopefully, the reader will comfort in 1 John 4:1–2, "Beloved, believe every spirit, but try the spirit whether they are of God because many false prophets have gone out." Note this Scripture assurance. At this point, the presentation will shift to a brief discussion of this writer's pathway to gerontology as an academic discipline.

As a professor, with centennial in sociology, history, gerontology, and death and dying, I headed the department of sociology, later served as academic dean of arts and sciences, and finally as interim chair of the department of history and political science at Albany State College/University in Albany, Georgia.

After the publication of my first book, *The Abundant Life*, and several additional books and after retirement, I am currently busy with a manuscript, *Beyond the Fear of Death*. It is my intention to complete this project by December 15, 2021. In the meantime, if interested, one can review my Amazon listing of published books—Dr. Eugene G. Sherman, Jr.

Reactions to Three Different Types of Death

A lingering death—bereavement of the survivor in three different forms: Physical, emotional, and intellectual.

A cancer death—anticipatory grieving.

An accidental death—shock and disillusionment.

Information Gleamed from Computer Search

1. Bible and the fear of death—100 verses
2. Matthew 10:28
3. Thanatophohia—the fear of death
4. <u>20 Major Philosophers and Their Big Ideas:</u>

1. Saint Thomas Aquinas	11. John Locke
2. Aristotle	12. Niccolò Machiavelli
3. Confucius	13. Karl Mark
4. Rene' Descartes	14. John Stuart Mill
5. Ralph Waldo Emerson	15. Friedrich Nietzsche
6. Michael Foucault	16. Plato
7. David Hume	17. Jean-Jacques Rousseau
8. Immanuel Kant	18. Jean-Paul Sartre
9. Suren Kierkegaard	19. Socrates
10. Cao Tzu	20. Ludwig Wittgenstein

CHAPTER 3

THE FEAR OF DEATH

The thought of death creates many different responses even with same person. Generally, the young child's view ranges from a myth, a poem, a play, or a mystery. Added to the poem, "Doctor, Doctor, will I die?"

The doctor responded, "Yes, my child, and so will I."

I was listening to a Christmas carol and thought of an imaginary response of the youngster. "So you do not believe in Christmas, nor you believe in Bible."

In awe, the doctor uttered, "Son, you had better let me send you home."

Well, that episode did not happen, but I created it. "The Bible, sir."

The doctor replied, "Let me hurry and finish with you, so you can go home."

Let it not be assumed that I, as the writer, am a nonbeliever in the Bible. Instead, the interested reader will find a section entitled *Biblical Living Guidelines* from the book of Psalms. Additionally, the current script has a section lifted from Google's section on the book of Psalms. A few selections from that reference are herein included in the current presentation. As earlier noted, Psalms contains many references to living, warning to humanity, and of particular indication on the aging process. Of special interest for this elaboration are humanity and life span (Psalms 90, 23; Ecclesiastes 12, 3–7).

In addition to section on *Biblical Living Guidelines,* the Psalm from contained herein, there is also a section lifted from the Bible where Scriptures certify the interrelation between life and death. Of particular interest, both in this discussion, are declining in strength, the losing of *grinders* or teeth as man goes to his long-anticipated home. Anyone familiar with these references should have no fear of death while getting ready for the Great Cross, but what are some reasons for the fear of death? They are numerous, some of which are:

1. Fear of the unknown
2. Fear of the pain of dying
3. Fear of the duration of the dying process
4. Fear of the reality of being dead
5. Fear of meeting adverse persons after death
6. Fear of the returning after death, but only as an invisible being
7. Fear of being unable to respond to negative information about our lifestyle
8. Fear of a lifestyle, after death, that prevails forever
9. Fear of inability to communicate with family members
10. Fear of possibility that post life experiences will be painful.

The fear of death greatly exceeds the ten reasons cited above. Hence, it is recognized that the fear of death is more than myths and legends. In the process of time, religious groups commenced to include time for ceremonies, ritual, home visitation, *wakes* at the home, religious facility, or a public facility. Of particular for this discussion is religion, and the Gullah People in Staple Island,

Georgia. I am authorizing and enclosing a photocopy from my book, *Black Religiosity*, page 21, to illustrate the commitment of a people to its deceased family members along with other members of this group.

Having *Death and Dying* both at the undergraduate levels, I chose to use some topics from the selected text. It was *Understanding Dying, Death, and Bereavement*, by Michael R. Leming and Dickinson. The press, electronic media, international travel, study, research, and unanticipated medical studies have been sources for generating theories, developing new medicines, and treatments and to enhance the quality of human life.

As a gerontologist, I am committed to research and therefore, recommend the four cited in the book by Leming and Dickinson. The four academic approaches are:

The biological approach—the human body
The psychological approach—the human mind
The anthropological approach—the human location
The sociological approach—the human groups

CHAPTER 4

SOME MYTHS ABOUT DEATH

Death is a reality that comes to every human being. It includes all forms of life: animals, trees, and several human creations—buildings and electronic gadgets. Mankind stands alone in recognizing the certainty of death. Accordingly, it becomes the task of people to recognize the ultimate reality of death.

Recognizing that death is certainty, humankind has developed a methodology that can be used to aid people in their effort to admit that death is a forthcoming reality. Hence, there has emerged a topic—*Some Myths About Death.*

Death can be a lingering or a swift event.
Death is easier as the person is at home.
Death is but a transition from time to eternity.
Death allows its choice of expired persons to return from their grave.

I experienced temporary death when I was coping with the Legionnaire disease here in Albany, Georgia. Let us remember the biblical statement, "A time to live and a time to die."

Death reminds us to anticipate as the old preacher called, "Get right with God before it's too late."

In the book by Leming and Dickinson, they wrote about death and dying. Their section was *The Meaning of Dying and Death*. The scholars listed nine ways by which the audience may be viewed at death. The referenced writers felt that the caregiver/family members should be observed.

Lastly, this book has three inserts that offer *Words of Wisdom: Learning the Dead, Word of Wisdom: Do not Disdain Death,* and *Words of Wisdom: Nothing Is Lacking in Death.*

CHAPTER 5

OBSERVATIONS

Contents:

Lecture Guides, Sermons
Personal Opinions of DOC
Professor, Lecturer, Pastor

The Certainty of Death

"And it came to pass, that the beggar died, and was carried by the angels into Abraham's bosom, and the rich man also died, and was buried" (Luke 16:22).

Death is an event that awaits every mortal person. It comes at all stages of life: birth, infancy, childhood, and adolescence. Death is an event that awaits every mortal person. It comes at adulthood, middle age, and old age. Death, as a topic, is taboo. People prefer not to talk about it. When death must be discussed, there is the tendency to use euphemisms such as expired, passed, crossed over Jordan, and gone to be with the Lord.

Prior to the late 1960s, the most prevalent attitude toward death was that of denial. Essentially, the belief was that access to competent medical service was a guarantee of delaying death. This attitude shifted from denial to acknowledgment after the publication of a book in 1969 by Elizabeth Kubler Ross entitled *The Meaning of Death and Dying*. The impact of that book led to the Hospice Movement and a more openness in discussing and planning for death.

In addition to the physical aspect of death, there is concern about the spiritual reality after death. This latter interest extends beyond medical knowledge and opens the window of religious teachings. There is considerable variation within the religious area regarding the afterdeath experiences.

Since the occasion today is a sermon instead of a class in death and dying, the focus will be directed to the Christian view of life after death. Hence, the sermon has been so entitled *Life after Death*. It will examine life after death as taught in the Holy Bible and preached by anointed persons who embrace, proclaim, and stand on the inerrant and infallible truth of the Bible. In this connection, the sermon will examine three facets of life after death, namely: the reality of death, preparation for death, and the life after death.

Prior to examining these facets of life after death, it is deemed appropriate to give a synopsis of schools of thoughts concerning death. All the schools acknowledge that death is universal, it is final, and it is nonreversible. From that point of commonality, the views become varied. Among them are assertions that include reincarnation, the soul migration, a state of neither existence nor nonexistence, multiple layers for both good and bad decedents, Sheol, immorality of the soul, and the life after death.

While all these views have ardent believers, no attempt will be made to evaluate them. Instead, the sermon will submit the New Testament view that there is life after death. Against this background, attention will now be focused on the earlier specified facets of the subject, the first of which is the reality of death. Both world and biblical histories document the reality of death.

The Bible disclosed that the first death was by murder, and it was caused by Cain's killing of his brother, Abel. That Sacred Book further contains an extensive list of persons who died; among the more highly profile deaths were Methuselah, Abraham, Moses, David, Jesus, Phillip, and Paul. In contrast, there were two persons who left the earth without experiencing death; they were Enoch and Elijah.

Beloved, there may be the yearning to leave this world without experiencing death, but that prospect is unachievable. Hence, every mortal should seek comfort in David's assertion, "Yea though I walk through the valley of death I shall not fear for thou art with me" (Psalm 23:4).

Concerns about the reality of death are interwoven with human existence. They are manifested in songs, poems, books, and nursery rhymes, one of which contains the words, "Doctor, doctor, will I die?" and the doctor's response, "Yes, my child, and so will I."

This somber fact leads to the second facet of the sermon; it is that of preparation for death. Friends, this is a task that confronts everyone, but too few persons take it seriously. There are three areas in which preparation for death should be made. They are social—mending broken relationship, planning funeral program, and giving away items.

The second area is in the legal arena. It includes making a living will, deciding on a power of attorney, and deciding on a person to make major medical decisions for you. The third, and most crucial area, spiritual—accepting Jesus as Lord and Savior. Beloved, this area is the crux of eternal life as taught in the Christian religion. Our Savior, Jesus, declared himself to be the resurrection and life (John 11:25) while Paul asserted that the Christian's hope for eternal life can only be anchored in the fact that God raised Jesus from the dead (Romans 10:9). Beloved, these Scriptural teachings lead to the last facet of the sermon, and it is life after death. The prospect of life after death is a widely debated topic. It has two extremes, the atheistic denial, and the Christian affirmation of the life after death. While according to the atheist privilege, for their incorrect view, the sermon will now document the reality of a life after death. It is based upon the account of Lazarus and Dives as told by Jesus. Friends, this is the only narrative in which Jesus gave the names of people. Hence, this is a real-life situation. Accordingly, everyone should read and believe the parable of Lazarus and the rich man because it clearly shows that there is life after death. This new life is in a nonphysical form, but it does include sensory awareness, a fact that will be revealed in the account of Lazarus and Dives. In support of this reality, kindly refer to your Bible from which a few points will be lifted to prove that there is life after death, and there is a sensory awareness in the new life form.

- First, the Bible tells us that there is differential living within the human group. Notice the rich man fair sumptuously whereas Lazarus lingered in poverty (Luke 16:19–21).
- Next death is a common denominator for all. Hence, the beggar died and later so did the rich man (Luke 16:22).
- Third, there were different destinations for the two; Lazarus was carried to Abraham's bosom while Dives ended up in the abyss of hell (Luke 16:22–23).
- Fourth, the Bible clearly shows that there is sensory awareness in the life after death. It seems that Lazarus was at perfect peace with his new life because there is no record of him complaining. Dives, in contrast, was using all of his sensory capacities to complain and beg for relief. Notice he saw Lazarus in Abraham's bosom, he cried unto Abraham for mercy, and he begged for Lazarus to come and dip the tip of his (Luke 16:24–25).
- Fifth, Abraham reminded Dives of his earthly prosperity and Lazarus's earthly sojourn in poverty. Further, he told

Dives that there is a gulf between Lazarus and himself that precluded Lazarus from coming should Abraham so order him (Luke 16:25–26).

- Last, Dives begged that Abraham would allow Lazarus to visit his five brothers and testify to them, lest they come into the place of torment (Luke 16:26). This plea was of no avail because Abraham told him that his brothers had Moses and the prophets and if they did not believe them, they certainly would not believe one rose from the dead (Luke 16:27–31).

In closing, my friends, the somber question facing each of us today is where do we stand with respect to our life after death? It is an avoidable fact that each of us will die, but that is just the beginning of perpetual existence in heaven or hell. Once we die, the destination is sealed. There is no changing our destiny regardless of prayers of our family, Church members, and others associated. But thanks be to God for his mercy, his Word, the Bible, his Son, Jesus, and his messages—the Gospel. There is no need for anyone to experience the agony of Dives; instead, by embracing Romans 10:9 and Revelation 2:10, we can experience the tranquility of Lazarus in our life after death.

Lecture Guide for Death and Dying

Prepared by Dr. E. G. Sherman, Jr. for use in his *Death and Dying* class at Albany State College/University.

Topic: Definitions of Death

I. Introduction

A. Death is a topic of historic concern for humanity.

B. The definition of death was expanded during the Death Education Movement to include a technical means for determining "brain death."

C. Two significant events that impacted the expanded definition of death were: the Tucker Case and the Harvard Medical School's report on death.

II. <u>Definitions of Death</u>

A. Text: "Death is when heartbeat and breathing stop."

B. Text (Kass): "The transition from the state of being alive to the state of being dead."

C. Shneidman in *Death: Current Perspectives* delineates five prototypes in defining death:

  1. The Kansas Law adopted in 1970
  2. The Capron and Kass Law in 1972
  3. The American Bar Association in 1975
  4. The Uniform Brain Death Act in 1978
  5. The America Medical Association in 1979

III. <u>Significance of Death within the Socio-Cultural Context</u>

A. Cause of death
B. Time of death
C. Place of death
D. Official certifying the death
E. Will
F. Individual responsible for final bill
G. Person in charge of funeral, body donation, and any other requirements.

The Problem of Death

> I am the resurrection and the life; he that believeth
> in me, though he were dead, yet shall he live.

> —John 11:25

The writings of Thomas Wolfe include a poem that addresses death. Commenting on death, Wolfe wrote, "Man loves life and loving life he hates death." This brief statement generally applies to most of our human race. There are some people, however, who chose to end their life through an act of suicide.

Death is a topic often avoided. It is reality largely dreaded, a thought frequently repressed, but a destiny that awaits every mortal being. Owing to the finality of death, humankind tries to place it within an acceptable social context. Hence, there are terms such as expired, passed, experienced the great transformation, and gone from labor to reward.

Throughout human history, people have had to face death. This fact is recorded in world history books and in the Holy Bible. Unfortunately, the history books describe only one type of death. They list causes of death, and they give a classification of deaths. But the history books view death as a final physical act. The Bible, in contrast, presents physical death as but one of three types of deaths. However, world history and biblical history both describe physical death as a problem, but the Bible offers a solution to the problem of death. Our sermon, in this connection, will examine the biblical teaching regarding death. It has been given the title *The Problem of Death*. The sermon will be anchored by three considerations:

1. An identification of the three types of death;
2. Some consequences of each type of death, and;
3. <u>Solutions to the problems of death.</u>

Prior to addressing the identified concerns, attention will be focused on the term death. It is a word used to denote the final separation of body from soul. Death is a topic that runs throughout the Bible. It is also a theme of songs, novels, and plays. Using the Bible as history, death occurred in the first family, when Cain murdered his brother Abel. From that episode onward, death was a recurring topic in biblical writings. Moses penned, "We spend our years as a tale that is told." In Ecclesiastes, it is recorded that there is a time to be born and a time to die. Job, an Old Testament patriarch, wrote "Man that is born of woman is of few days and full of trouble," and Saint Paul, a New Testament author, spoke of death as being absent from the body and presence with the Lord. These are but a few of the numerous biblical references to death, but they clearly show that death was a recurring interest during that time. In fact, Jesus himself spoke of death as noted in our text today, "He that liveth and believeth in me shall never die."

Since the Bible has so much to say about death, our sermon will analyze this reality under the heading *The Problem of Death*. The first consideration is that of the types of death. The Bible teaches that there are three types of death. They are physical, spiritual, and eternal. Every living person will experience the first type of death because the Bible warns, "Once to live and then to die." In many instances, people undergo spiritual death while being alive but not a peace with humankind nor with God. Anger, for example, is a type of spiritual death. The third type of death, also known as eternal, is the worst form because it leads to final existence in hell.

In sum, the Bible teaches that there are three types of death: Physical, spiritual, and eternal. Since all of us must, one day, face physical death, many of us may be in a state of spiritual death, and some of us—unless we straighten up—are bound for eternal death. Our sermon will now explore some aspects of each type, which is the second concern; what are the consequences of death?

A physical death. This type of death is the permanent separation of person from its body, material possessions, family, neighborhood, and the world at large. It is the most used from the word "death" in the Scripture. An example of this use is reflected in the parable of the foolish farmer, who heard the words, "Thy fool, this night thy soul is required of thee." He was separated from his large harvest of grains.

In writing to the Hebrews, Saint Paul reminded them that it is appointed unto men once to die, but after this, the judgment. Within that warning, Paul was sounding the need for spiritual peace with God and humanity. That statement leads to the second type of death; it is spiritual death which is the separation of the individual from God because it has sinned. Spiritual death entered the world with Adam and Eve. Since that time, spiritual death has always been a possibility even though Christ came into the world that we might have life and have it more abundantly.

Although this spiritual death has frightening consequences, it can be solved through prayer. One has but to earnestly cry unto the Lord, "Have mercy on me, a sinner saved by grace," and the forgiving Father will grant the request, and thereby remove the person from the destruction of spiritual death. If an individual neglects to seek forgiveness, it is headed for eternal death. This type of death is the second phase of spiritual death. It occurs when a person refuses to accept God's offer of salvation. Such a person will die eternally; that is, he will be separated from God forever.

John 8:24 warns of this danger. Therein, it is recorded, "I say therefore unto you, that ye shall die in your sins: For if you believe not that I am he, ye shall die in your sins." This prospect leads to the final consideration of our sermon—what is the solution to the problem of death? Referring again to the three types—physical, spiritual, and eternal—the Bible contains a solution for each type. First, is that of physical death. The Bible tells us in 1 John 3:1 that following physical death we shall have a glorious body like unto the Father. (Remarks about how his body was after the resurrection).

With respect to spiritual death, the Bible tells us that forgiveness is possible with the Father. Therefore, we should never be so ashamed of our transgression that we neglect to seek forgiveness with the Father. We should all seek to obtain forgiveness to avoid eternal death. This is the worst consequence of death.

Saint John 5:28 describes that destiny of those who experience eternal death. He wrote that they shall rise into the resurrection of damnation. Revelation 20:6 describes such persons as experiencing the second permanent death, namely, forever being separated from the Father and having to exist forever in hell. Cartoon humor and laughter (Tom and Jerry), Dante's "Divine Comedy" literature and intellectual speculation, Lazarus, and Dives—the biblical account. God spared not his angels.

Topic: Confronting, Living, and Enjoying the Later Years

I. Introduction

    a. Aging is a normal part of living.
    b. Aging is necessary for the infant to become an adult.
    c. Unless some unanticipated event, an accident occurs, aging will be the cause of death.
    d. Aging is not a disease, but it is a time when diseases are prone to occur.

II. The Study of Aging

    a. The study of aging is known as gerontology.
    b. The areas were established by Clark Tibbitts who named it gerontology.
    c. Gerontology is a post-World War II area of study.

   d. It is a national priority as evidenced by the White House Conferences on Aging, and later, the establishment of the Administration on Aging.

   e. Gerontology is now an academic area of study in which a degree can be earned.

III. <u>What Is Old Age?</u>

   a. The Bible: 70 (three scores and ten)
   b. Townsend: 60
   c. The Social Security Act: 65

IV. <u>The Areas of Aging</u>

   a. Biological
   b. Psychological
   c. Social
   d. Social Psychological

V. <u>Reacting to and Coping with Aging</u>

   a. The Disengagement Theory
   b. The Activity Theory
   c. The Ego Integrity vs Ego Despair

VI. <u>Needs of the Elderly</u>

   a. Economic
   b. Interactional
   c. Privacy
   d. Spiritual
   e. Physical Exercise
   f. Care Giver

VII. <u>Services for the Elderly</u>

    a. The RSVP/SOWEGA Council on Aging (432-1124)
    b. Meals on Wheels
    c. Senior Transportation
    d. Socially Sponsored Programs (a.k.a. Sorority)

VIII. <u>VFinances</u>

    a. Retirement Income
    b. Investment Income
    c. Social Security
    d. SSI
    e. Others

IX. <u>Health Care</u>

    a. Private Insurance
    b. Medicare
    c. Medicaid
    d. Disability

X. <u>Living Arrangements</u>

    a. Personal Residence
    b. With Family Member(s)
    c. Assisted Living Facility
    d. Personal Care Home
    e. Nursing Home

XI. <u>Personal and/or Communal Initiatives to Enhance the Joy of Living in the Later Years</u>

    a. Avoid or discontinue being a physical diagnostician.
    b. Take medications as prescribed.

    c.   Bever share medications with anyone.

    d.   Develop a *friendly visitor* phone calling to check on an associate and be checked on.

    e.   Develop a meaningful hobby—watering flowers, working in a small garden, reading, and listening to a religious program.

    f.   Exercise daily (at home or a gym) if physically able.

    g.   Take trips to the mall—but not alone—to just walk, sit, and enjoy the beauty of seeing life in action.

    h.   Maintain an active religious commitment both at home and a worship center.

    i.   Eat and drink foods, water, juices, and fruits on a regular basis.

    j.   Establish a routine for turning in at night, and do not become overanxious about being awake for short periods during the night.

    k.   View life as Maxwell's "Good to the last drop."

XII. Summary and Questions

Selective Dimensions of Aging

I. Introduction

II. Dimensions:

A. The "Personality" or total person

1. Innate characteristics—gender, race, eye color, IQ
2. Original culture—geography, family, language
3. Unique experiences—events known only to the person

B. Basic Needs

1. Food—baby, childhood, junk food, regular foods
2. Clothing—baby ware, adolescent styles, adult, work
3. Shelter—home, college, apartment, personal house

C. Socialization
1. Informal—acculturation, family, playgroups, relatives
2. Formal—school mates, college peers, workforce
3. Specialized occupational training—pilot, investigator

D. Economic Resources
1. Informal—family charities, soliciting
2. Formal—contractual, retirement, investment, SS /SSI

E. Adult Living Arrangements
1. Independent—personal apartment, house, others
2. Quasi-independent—residing in echo house, mobile home
3. Assisted Living—a facility that offers residence, food, medical transportation
4. Personal Care Home—a facility that offers family-like residence
5. Nursing Home—maximum services, food, bed services

F. Essential Planning
1. The Living Will—stipulation of use of body as donor or not
2. Medical Directive—authorizing one to make medical decisions
3. Economic—trust, deeds, will, administrator
   - Establishing funds for family, church, others
   - Charities
   - Conveying title to properties and other assets
   - Outlining how one plans possessions to be distributed
   - Person legally authorized to probate will and/or Estate

4. Funeral plans and expenses
5. Preneed arrangements
6. Prepare program for eulogistic services

Coping with the Reality of Aging
At
The AKA's Monthly Senior Luncheon

To _____ members of AKA, honorees, and guest, should there be any. I am honored to have been invited to share a few thoughts on aging. I am also grateful to this sorority for having recognized me as a friend of AKA and awarding me with a plaque. The shirt I have on today is the certification of my being properly dressed for the occasion. Additionally, I thank you for including me on your Christmas for 2019. Having so expressed my appreciations, attention will now be focused on a general age-related topic which is *Coping with the Reality of Aging*.

Following the close of World War in 1946 in America, I became aware of two new population realities, namely, the baby boom and the aging population. It is this second segment, aging that is the topic on this occasion. First, there was the recognizing of age sixty-five as old age, and next, there emerged a new area of study known as gerontology. My MA thesis was the nation's first study of elderly Negroes, as we were designated then, 1955. That thesis thrusted me into the national lime light. It was a new major then, from 1965–2002. It was a new profession for me, and since 2002, gerontology has become a new reality for me. Hence, I shall share a few of the academic, medical, and personal aspects of aging.

1. Aging is a forthcoming reality unless death occurs before age sixty-five.
2. While aging is a biological fact, reaction to it is first a psychological phenomenon.
3. Aging will inevitably bring about biological and psychological changes.
4. Ultimately, each person must decide for themselves just how to cope with aging.

5. Gerontologists have specified three major ways to cope with aging:
   - The Disengagement Theory—Stop everything.
   - The Activity Theory—Stay busy, but slow down.
   - The Reminiscence Theory—Daydreaming.

6. Aging ultimately impacts the total person (biological, psychological, and social).

7. Some recommendations and/or suggestions for coping with aging:
   - Maintain a positive outlook in life.
   - Monitor both the time of eating and what is being eaten.
   - Follow prescribed medication and be cautious about over the counter medication, and do not share medicines even with spouse.
   - Follow some type of exercise at least twice per week.
   - Keep alert of news and events each day.
   - Maintain a committed outlook on the Christian religion.
   - Utilize social services available for seniors.
   - Examples: The SOWEGA Council at our meeting the past Tuesday, several new programs were announced, one of which is Elder Nursing Home. I suggest that you might invite a representative to be a speaker at the February luncheon. Tell them, Dr. Sherman, "Told you to do it."
   - Establish a telenet with at least two people and call them each morning.
   - Thanks for the opportunity to lecture and to dine with you. An Irish benediction goes, "Top of the morning to you."

The Journey Called Life
We spend our years as a tale that is told.

—Psalm 90:9

Life has been variously described in terms of stages, periods, and categories. One authority listed four periods, and another specified eight, but this speaker—using the biblical reference to tale—views life as a story with three parts: A beginning, a middle, and an ending. Numerous are the writers of stories, countless are the number of stories, and varied are the themes of stories. Some stories are short, and others are long. Some stories cause laughter while others engender sorrow. Some stories are about people while others are the center of fictional characters. Irrespective of the story's length, impact, or character, it will include three parts: A beginning, a middle, and an ending.

The topic of life is a focus of study in psychology, medicine, literature, philosophy, and religion. Of particular concern for this afternoon is life from a psychological and a biblical view. The psychologists assert that life includes a series of developmental tasks. They vary greatly withing each of the three broads of adulthood, middle age, and old age. On the occasion, this afternoon's attention will be confined to old age—seventy and beyond. This is the period of some physical declines, some losses of family members, and an increasing tendency to think about earlier life experiences.

Let us now examine the Biblical teachings across the three categories of life. It teaches children to obey their parents, adolescents to grow up and put away childless ways, husbands to love their wife, and the elderly to trust in the Lord and be faithful unto death. In fulfilling this Biblical call, one needs to remember Psalm 90:10 that states, "The days of our life are three score and ten (70) and by reason of strength, they be four score years (80) they are soon cut off and we fly away."

The Bible also reminds us of an earlier time and how its change gradually has slipped upon us. That account is found in the twelfth chapter of Ecclesiastes. Let us notice them:

The keepers of the house shall tremble—our hands began to tremble; the grinders cease because they are few—our teeth are replaced with dentures; our looking in the window becomes darkened-failing eyesight; our hearing of voices and music is brought low-hearing loss and our fear of height and falling—causes a need for a walking cane or wheelchair.

So irrespective of our age, we are spending our years that is told. In view of this fact, we should heed the teaching found in Psalm 90:12, "Teach us to number our days that we may apply our hearts unto wisdom."

So as we, including myself, move toward the ending phase of our life story, let us mend broken fences, review our final business plans, avoid heartbreaking thoughts, and take comfort in our life's journey as was as Paul's message to Timothy, "I have fought a good fight, I have finished my course, I have kept the faith" (2 Timothy 4:7). Amen!

The Blessed Dead
Blessed are those who die in the Lord

—Revelation 14:13

The Bible is known as the Book of books. It tells of God's works and plans in times past, present, and future. The Bible has many themes and topics on the destiny of humankind. Probably, the most dreaded topic is that of death. Yet, this topic starts in Genesis and ends in Revelation.

Owing to the mystic step between life and death, humanity is urged to be ready for that unavoidable reality. The Bible, in this connection, describes those earlier prepared deceased persons as the blessed dead (Revelation 14:13). Our sermon today, in this connection, has been planned to commemorate the deceased members and family members of Institutional First Baptist Church. It was prepared under the title *The Blessed Dead*. The sermon will be undergirded by the following three objectives, namely: To *highlight* some biblical teachings on death, to *identify* three categories of the blessed dead, and to *characterize* the blessed dead.

Prior to addressing these objectives, brief attention will be given to some cross-cultural views and practices concerning death. The Hindus religion of India embodies a belief in reincarnation that occurs after death. The belief is that the deceased person will return to Earth in another form of animal life. The Buddhists of China are taught that death is the end of everything and that the human soul is absorbed into a state of nothingness. The Shintoism religion of Japan teaches that at death, the person's spirit becomes a spiritual overseer of its relatives. The Islamic religion of the Moslem world believes in seven heavens and seven hells.

Of concern today, however, is the religion known as Christianity. It stands alone as the religion whose founder did return and shall return to this Earth. Further, Christianity embodies the glorious notion of a life after death in which every person will either be forever with the Lord and with Satan (Matthew 25 and Revelation 20:12–15). Beloved, I am committed to the Christian view of death and its aftermath. Hence, I so live that my transition will be genuinely known as the blessed dead.

Against this overview of selective world religious views of death, attention will now be focused on the earlier defined objectives, the first of which is *to highlight some biblical views of death*. Three of the five poetic books—Job, Psalm, and Ecclesiastes—contain references to death. In the 14th Chapter of Job, his assertion about death is found. Job declared, "Man that is born of woman is of few days and full of trouble" (verse 1).

Ecclesiastes 12:5 makes a reference to humankind as going to its long home and the mourners go about the street. Psalm 90, a favorite eulogistic Scripture, Moses stated that, "The days of our years are three score years and ten and if by reason of strength they be four score years, yet is there strength, labor, and sorrow: For it is soon cut off, and we fly away. The text, also, addresses the topic of death by referring to it as the blessed dead."

This reference leads to the second objective which is to identify the different levels on which the blessed dead can be viewed. Although the Bible concerns on the third types, it is possible to conceive death from three views. The first type is that of being socially blessed. Herein, the deceased is thought of in terms of its earlier life impact on others. Good parents, for example, upon expiring will be remembered by their children as the people who contributed to their success. Likewise, committed teachers will be remembered as having been a blessing to their students. Caring pastors, in a similar manner, will have a record of blessing the congregation. There are but a few examples of how an expired person can be thought of as having been a social blessing during their lifetime.

The second type of blessed death is in the physical area. It includes traumatic events like a major accident, massive bodily injuries, agony of being kidnapped, prolonged torture as occurs in some confined settings, and freezing to death. These are but a few of emotionally draining physical conditions that cause the victim to view death as a physical blessing.

The third type of blessed death is spiritual death. It is the nexus of our sermon. This spiritual death is a major theme in the New Testament. While not being in a hurry to experience that blissful reality, the Bible-believing Christian is confident that a life exists on the other side of Jordan. Although this view is vividly asserted in the book of Revelation, let us first examine a few other Scriptures to gleam insights on experiences that await those who died in the Lord.

Friends, allow me to cite three biblical promises. *First*, John 14:2 promised a place for those who die in the Lord. Therein, it is stated, "In my Father's house are many mansions; if it were not so, I would have told you; I go to prepare a place for you; I will come again and receive you unto myself; that where I am, there ye may also be" (14:2–3). *Next*, the blessed dead are promised a robe as noted in Revelation 7:9; therein it is recorded a great multitude will be standing before the lamb clothed with white robes, and palms in their hand. *Third*, the blessed dead are promised a crown. Saint Paul not only saw the crown that awaited, but he declared a crown awaits all those who loved the Lord's appearance (2 Timothy 4:8).

In closing, my friends, the famous question of Nicodemus may well represent our inquiry, "Lord, how can these things be? What about this earthly tabernacle in which I am entrapped?" Readers, let us refer to 1 John 4:1–2 and note this Scripture assurance. "Beloved, believe every spirit, but try the spirit whether they are of God because Many false prophets have gone out."

At this point, the presentation will shift from an ongoing narrative to lecture guides. The first guide is entitled *Lecture Guide for Death and Dying*.

As results of medical technologies, it has become possible to prolong life, extending the trajectory, when the patient otherwise be classified as being dead. An example would be a patient being kept alive on a respirator, who otherwise would be pronounced dead. The Harvard Medical focuses on a medical model for use in certifying a person has expired. It consisted of: "(1) unreceptivity and unresponsively, (2) no movements or breezing, (3) no reflexes, and (4) flat electroencephalogram." (Atchley, p. 311).

There are many variables by which death can be classified. One of the criteria is known as NASH, a word that denotes natural, accidental, suicide, and homicide. Another variable that impacts death is known as demographics. This one encompasses age, race, gender, occupation, neighborhood, education, and general lifestyle. Death can further be examined in terms of the leading causes for its occurrence. According to a Center for Disease report January 19, 2012 the ten leading causes of death were:

Causes of Death	
March 16, 2021 for the book *Beyond the Fear of Death*	
Previously:	Currently:
Heart disease	Heart disease
Chronic lung disease	Cancer
Accidents	Covid-19
Diabetes Mellitus	Unintentional injuries
Pneumonia	Stroke
Cancer	Chronic lower respiratory diseases
Strokes	Alzheimer's disease
Alzheimer's disease	Diabetes
Renal disease	Influenza and pneumonia
Suicide	Kidney disease
	Suicide

Death is a topic that encompasses many questions or secrets, some of which are:

- What happens to the soul at death?
- Does physical awareness cease before death?
- Is there a period of inner peace before death?
- Is there a guardian angel to usher the person to eternity?
- Is there a level of awareness after death?
- Is there a reunion with earlier deceased family members?
- If possible, would the decedent return to Earth?
- Is there an impending judgment of the decedent?
- Does the good person receive more rewards than the bad person?
- Is there a power structure in the afterlife?

Seminar on Dying, Death, and Bereavement

I. <u>Introduction</u>

A. Overview
B. Selective concepts:
  • Dying, death, bereavement, thanatology, death education movement, life expectancy, life span, death with dignity, hospice.

II. <u>Parameters for Inclusions</u>

A. Classification by cause as established by the Uniformed Crime Division-NASH
B. The three historic perspectives of death:
  • Death as a natural event—until 1945
  • Death as a medical event—1946–1969
  • Death as a neo natural event—since 1970
  • Hospice and palliative care

C. Ten major causes of death in the USA:
  • Heart disease: 597,689
  • Cancer: 574,743
  • Chronic lower respiratory diseases: 138,080
  • Stroke (cerebrovascular diseases): 129,476
  • Accidents (unintentional injuries): 120,859
  • Alzheimer's disease: 83,494
  • Diabetes: 69,071
  • Nephritis, nephrotic syndrome, and nephrosis: 50,476
  • Influenza and Pneumonia: 50,097
  • Intentional self-harm (suicide): 38,364

D. Demographics associated with death:
E. Age, race gender socio economic status, education, occupation, neighborhood, religion lifestyle, family longevity

F. Determinants/Criteria for death
- Original mode—a non-reversible termination of heartbeat and breezing.
- Contemporary mode—a flat EEG.

G. The Governmental initiatives regarding aging and the later phase of life:
- The 1961 White House on Aging
- The Medicare/Medicaid legislation

H. The inclusion of Hospice Care under Medicare in 1982
I. The Dying Person:
Kalish has hypothesized a fivefold category of needs of the dying person:
- Economic
- Medical
- Familial
- Personal time to deny/accept the reality of dying
- Time to complete unfinished business

Elizabeth Kubler Ross:
- Denial
- Anger
- Bargaining
- Depression
- Acceptance

Cicely Saunders:

This individual had a passion for working with terminally ill patients first, as professional social worker, later as a nurse, and finally as a physician. She is the founder of the Hospice Program—it is a program of pain control for terminally ill patients.

There are three original types of hospice programs, namely: The hospital based, the free standing, and the cooperative type. Sources for hospice cost include Medicare. Some work-related include coverage, and private pay.

A. Planning for close of life
- Power of attorney
- Living will
- Major medical directive
- Pre needs funeral planning
- Will
- Disposal of assets will alive

The Survivor(s): Bereavements

The continuum of death experiences ranges from unanticipated to a lingering anticipation of the event. In all instances, the survivor(s) must respond to the death. This process of coping with a death loss is known as bereavement. Kalish has defined this experience as "getting over another person's death, a process that may be finished quickly or may never be finished."

Kavanaugh: Shocked Bereavement
- as a shock
- disorganization
- quasi normality
- recognizing the reality of death
- initiating a new lifestyle

Kalish: Bereavement Actions
- physical
- emotional
- intellectual

Worden: Bereavement/Mourning
- accept the reality of loss
- experience the pain of loss
- adjust to the new environment without the presence of the person of loss
- withdraw energy and reinvest in another person, if interested.

A. *Care Giving*

- The expiring person needs medical and an array of personal services. The providers can include family, volunteers, and home health personnel. It must be noted that respite time is included especially when the family is rendering the care giving.

B. *Dialogue and Adjournment!*

- Thanks for your attendance!

THE GERIATRIC CENTER
(Research, Education, and Consultation)
1012 Eighth Avenue, Suite C
Albany, GA 31701
(229 430-0000 Phone / Fax
LECTURE SERIES
ON
DEATH, DYING, AND BEREAVEMENT
By
E.G. Sherman, Jr.
Emeritus Professor of Sociology
Albany State University, Albany, Georgia
Pastor, Institutional First Baptist Church (Albany, GA)

Death, Dying, and Bereavement

I. Introduction

The historical American reaction to death and dying was that of death denial. That view was modified by the Death Education movement of the 1960s. Since that time, the emerging attitude is becoming one of reluctant acknowledgment of death as an inevitable reality.

II. Inventory of Personal Views on Death and Dying

  a. Your personal desired life span.
  b. Your definition of death.
  c. Your fears of death, if any.
  d. Your reason for participating in this seminar.

III. Western Conception of Death

  a. Pathology
  b. Taboo
  c. Enemy
  d. Challenge
  e. Legal transition

IV. The Evolving Attitude of Death and Dying in America

  a. Colonial to the Nineteenth Century
  b. The Nineteenth Century to 1960
  c. Nineteen Sixty-One to the Present

V. Changing Attitudes toward Death and Dying in America

  a. From denial to reluctant acceptance of death as the final stage of life.

b. From unrealistic reliance on medical technology for prolonging life to recognizing that it is finite in diagnosis and therapy.

c. From seeking merely to prolong life rather than to emphasize the quality of life.

d. From depriving the expiring patient of the right of choice in medical options to allowing this option.

e. From hospital confinement of terminally ill patient to the utilization of hospice programs, health agencies, family primary care givers, and respite workers to deliver services to terminally ill persons.

VI. Essential Concepts in the Study of Death and Dying

a. Thanatology
b. Dying trajectory
c. Death
d. Anticipatory grieving
e. Hospice
f. Grief
g. Bereavement

VII. Types of Death via Causes

a. Sudden and unanticipated traumatic deaths
b. Long term chronic illness death
c. Geriatrics (natural causes) death
d. "Acts of God"
e. Famines
f. Epidemics
g. Conquests

VIII. <u>Approaches for Studying Death and Dying</u>

    a. Biological
    b. Sociological
    c. Religious
    d. Literary
    e. Demographic

IX. <u>Perceptions of Death (by chronological order)</u>

    a. Nagy
    b. Infant
    c. Toddler
    d. Midler
    e. Leming
    f. Adolescence
    g. Young Adulthood
    h. Middle Aged Adulthood
    i. Older Adulthood

X. <u>Studies on the Fear of Death</u>

    a. Becker, "The denial of death is commonplace in our society...It is an expression of fear associated with the through of death."
    b. Leming—This author delineated eight types of death fear.

XI. <u>The Reality of Death and Dying</u>

    a. The Terminally Ill Death
        i. The primary caregiver's response is generally that of anticipatory grieving.

ii. The expiring patient, according to Elizabeth Kubler Ross, goes through five stages. Namely: Denial, anger, bargaining, depression, and acceptance.

iii. Affected family member experiences an initial shock. According to Robert Kavanaugh, the affected family members go through a series of progressive stages in the direction of ultimate reestablishment and the continuance with life.

XII. <u>Needs of the Dying Person</u>

a. *Doka (Spiritual)*
   i. To search for the meaning of death
   ii. To die appropriately
   iii. To find hope that extends beyond the grave

b. *Kalish*
   i. First, dying people have the same need for food, clothing, shelter, rest, and warmth that we all have".
   ii. The need of confidence that the family will not abandon them.
   iii. The opportunity to maintain their sense of self and self-esteem.

c. *Sherman*
   i. Economic
   ii. Medical
   iii. Familial
   iv. Personal time to deny/accept reality of death
   v. Time to complete unfinished business

XIII. <u>Stages of Awareness in the Dying Process</u>

    a. Closed
    b. Suspicion
    c. Mutual Pretense
    d. Open

XIV. <u>The Ethics of Dying</u>

    a. Traditional—Natural expiration
    b. Contemporary:
    c. Natural expiration
    d. Death with Dignity

The Living Will:
    i. Document
    ii. Implementation
    iii. Legal impediments

I. <u>The Place of Death</u>
    a. Within traditional medical facility
    b. Within hospice facility
    c. Within long term care facility
    d. At home

II. <u>Legal Documents Involving Death and Dying</u>
    a. Power of Attorney
    b. Will
    c. Major Medical Directive
    d. Living Will
    e. Preneed Plans

III. <u>The Role of Hospice in the Dying Process</u>
  a. Origin of Hospice
  b. Founder, Dr. Cicely Saunders of London, England
  c. Year 1967
  d. Purpose: To provide palliative care for terminally ill patients.
  e. The American Program, founded in Connecticut in 1982

Added a Medicare Hospice Benefit

  A. Type of Hospice Programs
    a. Free Standing Unit
    b. Hospital or Nursing Home Based Unit
    c. Hospice Corporation—Vista Health
    d. Care Corporation
    e. Miami, Florida

  B. The Hospice Team
    a. Physician
    b. Nurse
    c. Hospice Social Worker
    d. Chaplain
    e. Psychologist
    f. Various types of Aides
    g. Volunteers

  C. The Hospice Patients

Facing Death, and Dying at Peace

I. Introduction
    a.   Historically, America was a death denying society.
    b.   That view was modified by the Death Education Movement of the 1960s.
    c.   The contemporary view is that of death awareness.

II. Essential Concepts in the Study of Death and Dying

    a.   Thanatology
    b.   Dying trajectory
    c.   Anticipatory grieving
    d.   Dying
    e.   Death

III. The Fear of Death

Becker: "The denial of death is commonplace in our society as it is an expression fear associated with the thought of death."

Leming: Delineated eight types of death fear (See exhibit 1).

IV. Stages in the Dying Process

    a.   Elizabeth Kubler-Ross, a pioneer Thana ologist, studies terminally ill cancer patients and she concluded that most of them evolved through five stages, namely:
        i.   Denial
        ii.   Anger
        iii.   Bargaining
        iv.   Depression
        v.   Acceptance

V. <u>Needs of the Dying Person</u>

    a.   Economic
    b.   Medical
    c.   Familial
    d.   Personal time to deny/accept reality of dying
    e.   Time to complete unfinished business

VI. <u>Stages of Awareness</u>

    a.   Closed
    b.   Suspicion
    c.   Mutual pretense
    d.   Open

VII. <u>Legal Documents</u>

    a.   Power of Attorney
    b.   Will
    c.   Major Medical Directive
    d.   Living Will
    e.   Preneed Plans

VIII. <u>Hospice and the Expiring Patient</u>

    a.   Founder: Dr. Cicely Saunders in London, England.
    b.   Program: The emphasis is on pain control and maximum access to family members.
    c.   Congress added a Medicare Hospice Benefit in 1982.

IX. <u>The Survivor(s)</u>

    a.   Anticipatory grieving
    b.   Mourning
        i.   Responses: Physiological, emotional, and psychological.

      ii.   Tasks: To accept the reality of loss, experience the pain of grief, adjust to the environment—in which the deceased is missing—and withdraw emotional energy and reinvest it in another relationship.

   c.   Bereavement

X. <u>Support Groups</u>

   a.   Family Religious groups, peers, and professionals

Changing Attitudes toward Death and Dying

I. <u>Introduction</u>

II. <u>The Death Education Movement</u>

   a.   The 1961 White House Conference on Aging
   b.   Medicare/Medicaid Legislation
   c.   The death with dignity philosophy
   d.   <u>Elizabeth Kubler-Ross:</u> *Fivefold Theory of Dying*

III. <u>The Dying Person</u>

   a.   Theoretical view of Kubler-Ross
   b.   Essential needs according to Kalish
      i.   Economic
      ii.   Medical
      iii.   Familial
      iv.   Personal time to deny/accept reality of dying
      v.   Time to complete unfinished business

   c.   Cicely Saunders: Hospice founder
      i.   An alternative to the traditional in-patient expiration.
      ii.   A program of palliative care for terminally ill persons.

      iii.   An attitude of acceptance rather than denial of death.

IV. <u>The Professional Providers</u>

    a.   Physicians
    b.   Nurses
    c.   Chaplains

Reactions of Family and Friends to Death

I. <u>Introduction</u>

    a.   Normal human development and continued welfare require a multiplicity of stimuli. While the stimuli are numerous, and they are often evident at various age level, those in the latter years can be reduced to three types. The three stimuli are: Family, friends, and social support. The impact of these stimuli can be studied under the heading of *bonding.*

II. <u>Analysis of Bonding</u>

    a.   Definition
    b.   Types (3—see text pages 182-183)
    c.   Illustration—Bonding as a stool with three legs

III. <u>Analysis of the (Legs) Sources of Bonding</u>

    a.   The Family
        i.   Definition
        ii.   Types (2)
        iii.   Importance
        iv.   Stages

  v. Selective Characteristics: The couples, sandwiched generation, young adults, children as caregivers, siblings, grandparent (pp. 216–220).

 b. Friends
  i. Definition
  ii. Factors influencing friendship
   a. Age
   b. Gender
   c. Duration
  iii. Strengths and weaknesses of friendship
 c. Social Support
  i. Definition
  ii. Types
   a. Informal
   b. Formal
  iii. Strengths and weaknesses of the social support system.
  iv. The ideal system of family/social support networking.

The Aftermath of Death: (Survivors and Professionals)

I. Introduction

 a. Death causes a permanent break in the family and other groups
 b. Death can be studied from several perspectives, three of which are:
  i. The expired person, from a theological stance, has a different aftermath from the mortals.
  ii. The survivors, in contrast, experience a different aftermath following death of a family member or a significant other.

iii. The Professionals, in the meantime, are expected to render compassionate, competent, and ameliorative services to the survivors.

II. <u>Dimensions of the Aftermath of Death</u>

    a. A. Prior to the death of a lingering patient, the family members are prone to experience a feeling known as anticipatory grieving.

    b. Following the expiration of the patient, the family members commerce to experience reality grieving.

    c. This reality grieving is also known as traditional grieving.

    d. There is another aspect of reality grieving known as disenfranchised grieving.

III. <u>The Aftermath of death (survivors) can be viewed under three major headings as noted below:</u>

    a. *Bereavement.* The process of coping with and attempting to get over the death of a family member or significant other; it is the process during which the person is commencing to make efforts to "pull together: the broken ends and get on with the remainder of life.

    b. *Grieving.* "A response to bereavement; it is also how the survivor feels. It is also how the survivor thinks, eats, sleeps, and makes it through the day".

    c. *Mourning.* "The culturally patterned expression of the bereaved person's thoughts and feelings".

    d. The human responses to these three conditions vary along several demographic lines, some of which are: age, gender, marital status, religion, and socioeconomic status.

    e. Lopaka, in his study of bereavement, hypothesized the existence of three different reactions, namely:

    i.   Physical—shortness of breath, sighing, loss of energy, upset stomach.

    ii. Emotional—anger, depression, anxiety, outburst of anguish.

    iii. Intellectual—the purification stage in which the survivor tries to forget faults of the deceased and concentrate, rather on the positive features.

f. Mourning can be studied from two perspectives; they are:

    i.   *Non*-pathological. The normal signs of bereavement, efforts to stay the course, and making some progress with the continuance of life.

    ii. Pathological. Preoccupation with thoughts of the deceased person, periodic times of excessive outcries, and a reluctancy to acknowledge that death has cause a permanent separation between the survivor and the expired individual.

g. Four tasks of mourning according to Worden:

    i.   Accept the reality of loss.

    ii. Experience the pain of loss.

    iii. Adjust to the environment in which the deceased is missing.

    iv. Withdraw emotional energy and reinvest it in another relationship (or self-preoccupation).

Remember the statement: A time to live and a time to die.

CHAPTER 6

SOME RELIGIOUS PERSPECTIVES ON DEATH AND DYING

Sociologists and other social scientists view human society as consisting of five major institutions. They are family, religion, education, government, and economy. Each of these institutions performs an essential function for the welfare of humankind. It is therefore appropriate that this book will include a chapter on some religious perspective on *Death and Dying*.

Since the author earlier noted his university teaching of a course on *Death and Dying*, using as a text, *Understanding Dying, Death, and Bereavement*, a decision was made to use the list of religions in that book. The religions listed were Judaism, Christianity, Islam, Hinduism, and Buddhism. Each of these religions will be defined, but Christianity will be analyzed extensively.

These religions differ in founder, geographical location symbol(s), teachings, and intent. Hence, they will be highlighted as per founded in a Google search.

Religion

This word is pronounced ri-li-gion. It refers to the belief in and worship of a supernatural power, especially God or gods, a particular faith or style of worship. As noted earlier, this chapter will briefly identify the often recognized the five historical Western religions but place major emphasis on Christianity. The first religion herein included is Judaism. It is the monotheistic religion developed by the ancient Hebrews. Islam will be highlighted next, instead of Christianity. Islam—the followers of Islam are called Muslims—embody the Five Pillars. Hinduism is an Indian religion. It is the third largest religion in the world. Lastly, the Christian religion is discussed.

According to the Holy Bible, Jesus is the founder of the Christian religion (Matthew 16:16–18). "Upon this rock, Peter, I will build My church." This Abrahamic monotheistic religion, the largest in the world, is based on the life and teachings of Jesus Christ. Furthermore, it is anchored on five theological assertions:

1. Virgin birth of its Founder
2. The Trinity
3. Necessity for the Cross
4. The Resurrection and the Second Coming, and;
5. The Inspiration of the Scripture.

As used in this discussion of religion, it encompasses several functions. It gives meaning and purpose to life, reinforces social unity and stability, serves as an agent of social control, promotes psychological and physical well-being, and may motivate people to work for positive social change.

Sadly, there are instances where so-called religious leaders organize cults, two of which were highly publicized in recent times, namely: Jonestown Massacre, 2020, and Waco, Texas, 1993. Another instance are the two church shootings: the 1963,

16th Street Baptist Church in Birmingham, Alabama with four deaths, and the 2012, Emanuel AME Church, Charleston, South Carolina with nine deaths. As noted earlier in this chapter, there are five religions noted therein and viewed as social institutions. Prior to discussing them, two dimensions of this concept are essential—definition and function.

By definition, "A social institution consists of a group of people who have come together for a common purpose. These institutions are the social order of society, and they govern the behavior and expectations of individuals."

Secondly, the functions of social institutions are:

1. To help the individual cope with the demand of living.
2. To identify sources from agencies from which the individual/group may seek assistance.
3. To help agency maintain records on its citizens.
4. To assist new persons in adjusting to their location.

As earlier indicated, at the end of this discussion is a collection of photographs of the Louisiana Black School System that was often housed in the Black Church. (Here it is!)

The Divine Provision: Peace or Punishment
(Romans 2:6–8 KJV)

When I was an Associate Professor of Sociology at Florida A&M University, I was shocked to hear an elderly start his address with the words, "Fools rush in where wise men fear to tread..." I, like him, am now in the waning years of both my publishing and traveling years, and prone to tackle fewer challenging task. But when I notice the political arena, the unfair articulations of senior officials, unequal treatments against people of color, and the list goes on and on. As I prepare this sermon, the voting is going on, but through this sermon, like Isaiah 62:1, for Zion's sake (and all those listed above), I will not hold my peace!

Accordingly, I shall commence with a twofold objective, namely, to complete the sermon for June 27 and to integrate this sermon with the conclusion of chapter 7 of the book, *Beyond the Fear of Death.*

Although religion was a recurring topic in the implementation of slavery in America, it was distorted yet the helpless people found methods to learn of, teach about, and pray to God.

Now taking a quantum from this earlier presentation to the sermon for today entitled, *The Divine Provision: Peace; or Punishment (Romans 2:6–8 KJV).*

The focus will now shift from a theological to a pragmatic discussion. It will encompass a threefold discussion, all religious in intent:

1. A religious "Fireside Chat;"
2. Some religious functions in human existence, and;
3. <u>Conclusion of chapter 7 in the fourth coming book,</u> *Beyond the Fear of Death.*

The religious presentation for the 27<u>th</u> (morning worship) was labeled, *A Fireside Chat.* It will be presented under Romans 2:6–8. The message subject will be, *The Divine Provision: Peace or Punishment.* To capture the youth, it was noted that this reality occurs after death! Hence, it can be remembered as heaven or hell. When I was... (See page 4).

Functions of Religion

1. The role and value of religion in human interactions. People recognize that God created the heaven, the Earth, humankind, the duration of life, and the final placement of every decedent.

2. Religion is generally included in family life: Birth, birthday parties, graduation events, marriage, church membership, family prayer, death/burial, and other events.
3. Religion is often a theme of books authored by this writer; they are found on Amazon. (Dr. E.G. Sherman, Jr.)
4. <u>Biblical Guidelines for Daily Living with Eugene Sherman191/Daily Spark with Dr. Angela.</u>

The subject evolved from this pastor's multi-earned academic degrees, graduate teaching, published books, and being concerned about the widespread inequities imposed on people of color! My mind commenced to wonder, has God prepared a place for humankind? After death, where the decedent shall be in everlasting, in *peace or agony! heaven or hell*! Therefore, I will share this biblical certainty with humanity.

Oh, there are people who will criticize this speaker for the subjects of the past two Sundays, and now say he is neglecting to build a message about justice and George Floyd. That criticism, if made, is okay because I preach under Divine guidance. Hence, I will use the subject, Peace or Agony: Heaven or Hell (Revelation 2: 6–8). This subject describes the final reality for every decedent. It was created by God, it becomes a reality after death, in short, it is heaven or hell!

Following my usual sermon format, three objectives will anchor this sermon, namely: Divine oversight and personal responsibility, time sequence personal responsibility, and biblical verification of the certainty.

Scriptures:	In the beginning, God	Genesis 1:1
	The Lord is my Shepherd	Psalm 23: 105
	Touch not my anointed	Psalm 105:15
	Your thoughts are not as my	Isaiah 55:8–9
	Oh, wicked man	Romans 7:15–20

Objectives:	Divine Oversight/personal responsibility	
	Time sequence/now and then	
	Biblical human certifications	
	Lazarus and Dives (Luke 16:19–31)	

A. Benediction

B. Conclusion: General implication and appeal to listener.

Social Institutions and Their Functions

Generally, the following are the functions of social institutions in societies of the world:

- Reproduction. The *institutions* reproduce human race, goods, services, traditions, and all other patterns of *social* life
- Socialization
- Sense of Purpose
- Preservation of *Social* Order
- Transmission of Culture
- Personality Development

Christianity

As noted earlier in this chapter, there are five religions classified as Western, but only one of them, Christianity, will be used in this presentation on *Beyond the Fear of Death*. As the reader will discern, the discussion will have a heavy African-American focus since it seeks to inform readers of "stormy pathway of ancestors and even the current injustices we yet encounter, but yet having faith to 'lean and depend on the Almighty God.'"

There were six hurdles that the WASP used to control us then and now: Terrier, lynching, denial of education, raping, no formal education, no formal religious experiences.

But God was not forgetful of his enslaved children's cry! Hence, He gave us an underground church, an underground railroad, the Negro Spirituals, and later, our own little churches *in the valley by the wildwood.* In later years, our church forefathers would establish a school at the little church. I was blessed in the later years to sit in on one of those churches/schools. The event was held in Kinder, Louisiana, the place where my sister-in-law, Birdie C. Sherman, had attended. Her husband, Louris W. Sherman, a brother of mine, had invited me over to deliver the dedication of that facility.

Taking a quantum leap, I now turn to historical value of the Negro church. It built schools. Recently Howard University was featured on the national news beat. But it must never be forgotten of the importance of churches and schools in our struggles.

Now the focus will shift to the behavior of our contemporary (educated, affluent, and altruistic persons) who seek to keep alive memory of our pathway as death *calls its roll.* We have memorials, wakes, funerals, Omegas, home sittings the night before the funeral. Many years ago, there was a general house cleaning the day after the funeral, but it must be remembered that death occurred at home.

In closing this chapter on religion, I, as an Elderly Minister, must share some exploitations of worshipers by unscrupulous "preachers" I have heard so-called faith healers guarantee a cure, relief of pain, or finding a companion. Occasionally, some of those people who have watched my website for the Sunday broadcast (Biblicalechoes0) contact me and ask for a medical healing. Unfortunately, I must tell them that my ministry makes no financial promise of granting their request. Instead, my approach is to encourage them to pray, keep their *money* and read—if interested—my pamphlet on The book of Psalms included in chapter 9 of this study on *Beyond the Fear of Death*.

As noted earlier in this chapter, the dedication was at the church where my younger brother is Chairman of the Board, and his wife attended that Black Church/School for her undergraduate schooling. The facility was in Kinder, Louisiana, and named Morehead Church. I was recently sharing this experience with members of my family in our regular phone conference, and one of our retired sisters, Arkansas A&M University's Academic dean said, "Why did you not include our family except our youngest family member? You should be proud to share with your readers our childhood educational experience in a one teacher church/school." It was an oversight, and thanks to the family, I am now fulfilling the commitment with facts, accomplishments, and retirements.

Thanks, family!

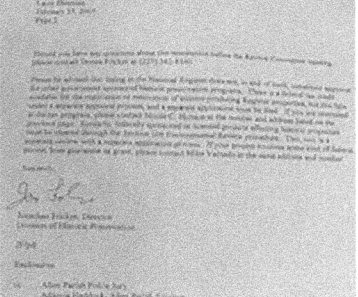

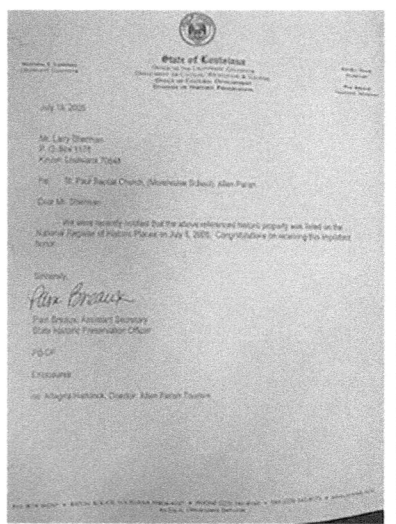

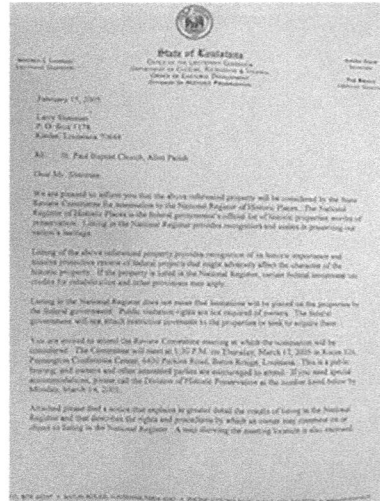

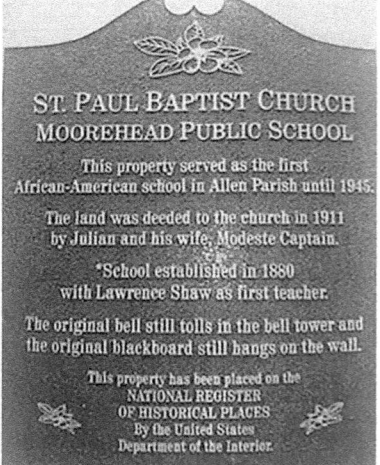

Our Sherman family resided in Rural Grady County, Georgia. This was during the early 1920–1950. As law abiding inhabitants, our education was conducted in a rural church/school, and it was known as Saint Stephens Elementary School. Both the church and the school were owned by the church members. It was a one-teacher facility who taught all classes and was supported with funds supplied by the Grady County Board of Education. We, the students, had to walk to school and back home at the close of the school day. Yet, the students and committed parents, relatives, and church members all united to help in the education of the children. In closing, we, the students, of the church/school complex, sponsored by Saint Stephens Missionary Church, thanked God for the Divine guidance shown to the oppressed people!

Therefore, we are presenting notes from the book of Psalms.

CHAPTER 7

BIBLICAL LIVING: GUIDELINES FROM THE PSALMS

Beyond the Fear of Death

Since we have decided to make everything that follows part of a pamphlet, start with notes from the book of psalms.

Notes from the book of Psalms

Introduction

This pamphlet, or short essay, emerged from the authors' desire to share some professional views on the contemporary concerns in the world. This discussion is nonmedical but warrants some thought and prayer.

Having been a Sunday school teacher, an academic dean, state/ theological, pastor, and publisher of two of my five books, two of which are youth focused and one in the process entitled, *Beyond the Fear of Death*, this writer is cognizant of the range of questions, doubts, and the forthcoming actuality of the event. Hence, this writer felt the need to respond to these and other inquiries.

Part 1
Selective Chapters from Psalms

Selective books, pages, and applications to address humanity.

Life is a sojourn between birth and death. Its pathway includes numerous and varied experiences. Individuals differ in their approach to life; some move blindly along from day to day, some plan for the next day during the evening or early night, some read the daily devotion, some wear symbols of the crucifix, some read the daily horoscope, some carry omens, and some have no concerns about events of the day. Hence, they like the proverbial Old Man River—they just keep rolling along!

This book has been prepared to offer some guidance, hope, and confidence while traveling on the road of life. It consists of selective chapters from the book of Psalms, the King James Version. The chapters were selected to address lingering questions, desires, guidelines, and anticipations throughout the duration of life.

Starting with thoughts about creation (Psalms 19), the selected chapters stretch across an array of human concerns and ends with the termination of life (Psalms 90).

Admittedly, the selections chosen for inclusion in this book reflect more the author's training, ministerial experiences, and insights gleamed from extensive and continuous reflecting on the sojourn of life and, at the same time, striving to unlock the biblical teachings as found in the book of Psalms.

The heavens declare the glory of God (Psalms 19).

Who owns the world? (Psalms 24).

Who created humankind? (Psalms 8).

Is it possible to hide from God? (Psalms 139). Where shall I flee from?

Who is the blessed person? (Psalms 1).

Is there divine leadership and provision? My shepherd (Psalms 23).

What is the expected life span…the days of our years are? (Psalms 90).

How to deal with adversarial persons (Psalms 37).

Facing terror (Psalms 91:5–7).

Who shall Dwell with the Lord? (Psalms 15).

What does the fool say about God? (Psalms 14).

What is God to the believer? (Psalms 18).

What is the source of the believer's light? (Psalms 27).

What is the value in forgiveness of sin? (Psalms 32).

What is the destiny of the wicked? (Psalms 37).

The advantage of waiting on the Lord (Psalms 40).

How is cleansing attained? (Psalms 31).

Personal guilt and desire for to be purged (Psalms 51).

Disregard of God (Psalms 53).

Joyfully honoring God (Psalms 66).

It is a good thing to give thanks unto God (Psalms 92).

A call to worship God (Psalms 95).

A call to praise God (Psalms 100).

A commitment to holy living (Psalms 101).

A prayer to be heard (Psalms 102).

Thanksgiving for mercy (Psalms 103).

Thankfulness for divine provisions (Psalms 107).

Praise the Lord for his care (Psalms 111).

The truth of the Lord endureth forever (Psalms 117).

God's sustaining power (Psalms 121).

Seeking comfort in the sanctuary (Psalms 122).

Acknowledging deliverance from enemies (Psalms 124).

Vanity in building without God's blueprint (Psalms 127).

The value in unity (Psalms 133).
Thanking the Lord for past and present blessings (Psalms 136).
Mourning while in captivity (Psalms 137).
The ever presence of God (Psalms 139).
Seek a divine refuge (Psalms 142).
A prayer to do thy will (Psalms 143).
The blessing in trusting in God (Psalms 146).
Great is the God of power (Psalms 147).
Join creation in praising God (Psalms 148).
Pleasing the Lord through praises (Psalms 149).
Let everything that has breath praise the Lord (Psalms 150).
Selections continued: 53, 54, 66, 77, 90, 91, 92, 95, 100, 103, 111, 116, 120, 121, 122, 124, 127, 133, 136, 139, 147, 150... Others: 21, 17, 96.

Part 2
This is the beginning of the next focus of
this brief presentation on Psalms.

Information Gleamed from Computer Search

This section is based on the book of Psalms and intended to help the reader to understand and utilize teachings from Psalms in personal living and helping humanity to understand and utilize God's messages to his readers and believers.

In my Google search of Psalms, I am herein including some teachings regarding this book. What does the book of Psalms teach us?

Part 3
The Author's Selection of Topics in Psalms

1. "What does the book of Psalms teach us?"
2. Many of the Bible's main ideas are echoed in the Psalms.

3. Praise, thankfulness, faith, hope, sorrow for sin, God's loyalty and help.
4. The Psalms teach us how to pray.
5. The Psalms teach us the importance for using them.
6. Five things the Psalms teach us about being honest to God.
7. What does the Bible say about parents and children?
8. What does the Bible say about children teaching parents?
9. Psalms for Families: Devotions for all ages, introduction…
10. Eighteen best Bible verses about family: Family Bible verses…
11. Twenty Bible verses about family: Scripture for solving family…
12. Twenty meaningful Bible verses about children: What the Bible …
13. The work of marriage, raising children, and caring for …
14. What does the Bible say about raising children? …
15. What does Psalms teach about family, children and about parents?
16. Ten vital Bible verses for parents: Disciple.
17. Scriptures on family: Scriptures on family.
18. Bible verse about parents love for child.
19. Bible verses about parents and child.
20. Scripture of family togetherness.
21. What does the Bible say about family relationships?
22. Importance of family in the Bible.
23. Scripture about family turning against each other.
24. Examples of family problems in the Bible.
25. Bible verse about family happiness.

Thanks to God for the idea of creating a short document focused on *the book of Psalms.*

End of Presentation: *Beyond the Fear of Death*
Presentation on "Care for the Caregiver"

Modality of Presentation

I. <u>Introduction</u>

Aging, prolonged illness, and physically challenged individuals pose a problem for many people, who are responsible for their welfare. These realities impact the lives of persons under whose care they must depend. Admittedly, the magnitude of the phenomenon is increasing, and currently, engendering problems for many persons, who, by choice or necessity, must assume the caring functions for the person(s).

Ongoing obligations and expectations of such a person, often designated as the caregiver, place incessant demands on that individual. Yet that caregiver, often a family member, has needs that remain unmet.

II. <u>Some Conceptual and/or Theoretical Parameters</u>

Caregiver. One who has the responsibility for the welfare of another person(s).

Types of caregivers:

- *Familial.* Related by blood, marriage, or adoption
- *Volunteer.* Church, neighborhood, or friend
- *Professional.* Self-employed or personnel agency

Uniqueness of the familial caregiver:

- An array of needs: economic, social physical psychological, and spiritual.
- The *real* caregiver (often round the clock).

A. Selective concepts:

- Respite, learned helplessness, affective neutrality, anticipatory grieving, bereavement, readjustment

I. <u>Selective References</u>

A. <u>Atchley, Robert C.,</u> *Social Forces and Aging ...*
B. <u>Belsky, Janet,</u> *The Psychology of Aging*
C. www.aging notes.com
D. The R. Carter Institute of Mental Health, *Caring for You, Caring for Me.*

CHAPTER 8

LIVING DURING LATER MATURITY

I. <u>Introduction</u>

    1.   Selective concepts—old age, later maturity, senescence

    2.   Historical facts—Townsend, Roosevelt, Johnson, Nixon

II. <u>Some highlights on living during later maturity</u>

    1.   The four theories of aging

        1. *Biological.* Changes in the body.

        2. *Social.* Changes in associates.

        3. *Social psychological.* Attitudes and self-image.

        4. *Psychological.* Changes in capacity to remember.

    2.   Pattern of reacting to aging

        1. *Disengagement theory.* throw in the towel of work.

        2. *Withdrawal theory.* focusing on self per se.

        3. *Activity theory.* finding something to do.

    3.   Problem areas

        1. *Income solvency.* Adequate funds for survival travel

2. *Health*. Enhancing personal independence
3. *Losses*. Family, friends, associates
4. *Age Encroaching Problems*. Systemic
5. *Transportation*
6. *Personal Care*. Home as long as possible

III. Some suggestions and/or recommendation for living during later maturity.

1. *Psychological*. Maintain a positive image of self
2. *Social contacts*. Develop a few contacts for conversation
3. *Religious*. Use exiting sources worship, tv, reading…
4. *Health*. Keep a close watch on health status
5. Avoid buying into tv advertised medications.
6. Do not share medications with family nor friends.
7. *Form a dual friendly visitor arrangement*. Call each other in the morning to make sure each is alive.
8. *Calendar*. Keep one on display and check every day to help maintain mental alertness.
9. *Home security*. Keep keys in a regular place and avoid too much security door thereby making it difficult to escape in case of emergency.
10. *Smoke detector*
11. *Security system*
12. *Beware of financial scams*
13. *Do not accommodate beggars*. Home/street
14. *Avoid late night travel*.

Living during later Maturity

Life is but a short sojourn between birth and death. It starts with a struggle to activate the breezing process and ends when the available medical technology is no longer capable of sustaining life. Life's duration is highly variable with the human group. Hence, death can occur before birth or at any age thereafter. However, it is more prevalent in the elderly population. Since the fact is unchangeable, the challenge is for the elderly, including myself, to seek, utilize, and follow a lifestyle that will, hopefully, prolong life. Accordingly, this brief presentation will cite a few facts, submit a few recommendations, and offer a few encouraging words for living during later maturity.

I. <u>A few historical facts: Legislation to aid the elderly:</u>

    a. Under the leadership of President Roosevelt, Congress passed the Social Security Act in 1935.

    b. Under the leadership of President Johnson, Congress passed the Medicare Act in 1965. The Medicaid Act was later added as an Amendment to the Social Security Act.

    c. Under the leadership of President Nixon, Congress Passed the Cost of Living Act that went into effect in 1975.

CHAPTER 9

SOME IMPACTS OF DEATH ON FAMILY AND OTHERS

An often neglected, sparely mentioned, and or omitted topics death involving death in the family presentations lectures. This approach emirates, I, from the general practice of keeping certain types of information from children especially that thought to bring grief, fear, and worry about their present and long-term welfare.

Death brings both a thought and challenge to children. When there is but one child, the worry is more traumatic because it has none to *talk* with. It is nonetheless an individual with human desires. According, it is entitled to communication about multiple questions. This is where family, worship center, social service agencies, and other committee people can and should offer their experiences. Essentially, the young child is shocked by the death and yearns to know why it happened and what is going to happen to them!

We parents, professionals, family life counselors, members of the Clergy, family members of the child/children where the death has occurred. It must be recognized, however, that youngsters experience in living often is short, self-interpreted, and remembered. To this end, siblings, parents, and other persons of contact—all must be ever mindful of this reality. Job 14 says, "Man that is of woman is few days and full of trouble." In another setting, in Psalms 90:7–12, a lengthy admonition is found. There are many other biblical references to death, but I will close this discussion with the heavenly promise to all who were committed to the Lord Jesus (Revelation 2:10).

1. Why did the death have to occur?
2. Why do good little children have to die?
3. Do children go to heaven or hell when they die?
4. Will our dead family members greet us when we die?
5. What will happen to our possessions especially toys?
6. Do we have to hold a funeral?
7. Do the Lord care about our pain, sadness, and disappointment?
8. What about those gambling crooks who seem to have no concerns about dying, yet they are quick to kill others?
9. How might our family tell *those* gamblers about the pain it causes?
10. Funeral experiences of the author: Person born in rural Grady County, Georgia and received full tuition and transportation fees for graduate studies at Southern Illinois at Carbondale, Illinois and the Gullah/Geechee cultures documented in part of my book, *Black Religiosity. A Biblical and Historical Perspective*, p. 21. (*See photo of book below*).

CHAPTER 10

IS THERE A LIFE AFTER DEATH?

This presentation is a paradoxical one to write, owing to several views that Aeneid focuses on, a reality that everyone will or have encountered. This writer has taught on the subject as an academic professor, lectured at several locations, delivered sermons on this. As he humorously said, "I have seen funeral homes, graves, but never seen a person who returned from being dead."

Later in the presentation, I shall discuss the so-called near-death experience. In fact, I experienced one of those realities when I was in the hospital here in Albany, Georgia.

In the meantime, the focus is on commercialization of death, as seen in the funeral industry, cemeteries, family-owned plots, religiously owned plots, government-owned plots, and hospice/personal care homes.

The array of medical facilities provides maximum access to doctor prescribed medications, over the counter medications, along with health-related items. Sadly, the access and availability can be a problem for many consumers without insurance or impeded by limited funds.

There are three options widely used to cope with financial limitations: Neglect getting the prescription filled, use family/neighbor's medication, or purchase medication from a street vendor. This writer recommends none of the above!

There is a cadre of people known as *Root Doctors*, offering services both in their office and years ago on the back of a wagon. What is needed is a functioning *Congress*. Items to include are suicide, over-the-counter medications, excessive alcoholic consumption, pursuing non-safe actions, along with other personal factors. There are other sources of information and/or actions regarding illness and death. Among the sources are religious healers, street peelers, etc., commercialization of the funeral industry as seen in the funeral homes, graveyards—church-owned, family-owned and governmental owned as reflected in the recent broadcasts of military and/or political officials, especially during the month of December 2021.

Now I shall discuss my near death experience. First, I must indicate biases regarding this event. They are three. I was a professional Gerontologist and taught *Death and Dying* at Albany State University, Albany, Georgia. I am a theologian and retired executive academic dean at Bethany Divinity College and Seminary in Dothan, Alabama, and lastly, I am writing a book entitled *Beyond the Fear of Death*. In the meantime, I shall present my near-death experience.

First, I was seriously ill and confined to the hospital Phoebe Putney Memorial Hospital, Albany, Georgia. Later that afternoon, when the doctor arrived, I heard his yell, "Clean this room." He came over to my bed and asked, "How are you?"

I do not recall ever having responded. Instead, I seemed to have felt a jolt, a then failing of peace as my body was floating somewhere. At the end of the float, I seemed to be in comfort, peace happiness, and no pains. That period of tranquility, I do not know its duration, but I vividly remember the call, "Gene, you are going to live, and return to your family, teaching, church, and neighborhood." That voice joyfully said, "Let us go now."

And I seem to recall uttering, "Thank you," and felt blessed.

After being discharged from a nursing home in Albany, Georgia and getting access to my library, I did extensive research on near death experience, and in the process, I came across Dr. Jack Kevorkian and highlighted his professional life, and experiences. He was often called "The Death" because he rejected NDE and offered instead legal euthanasia and assisted suicide. This procedure was condemned by the Bible, "Thou shall not kill," and in 1997, the U.S. Supreme Court ruled that "Americans do not have a Constitutional right to doctor-assisted suicide" (Kevork).

CHAPTER 11

DIVINE PROTECTION

The Lord bless you and keep you.
—Numbers 6:22–27

The human group is marching from time to eternity.

Many members of humanity, some may have been in our family to cross over into immorality during the past year, 2021. Their departure invoked grief and loneliness within their immediate family, but—in a larger sense—it reminds us, as mortals, that the awful day will surely come when we, too, must stand before our judge. So as we engage in this corporate worship, let us unite in giving thanks to the Almighty God for our past and present blessings.

Let us, further, utter prayers for guidance and protection each day and for the remainder of our Earthly sojourn. Such a request is biblical sound as is documented in so many different scriptural references. Psalm 48:14 tells us that he will be our guide; Psalm 91:4 reminds us that he shall cover thee with his feathers, and under his wings shalt thou trust; his truth shall be thy shield and buckler. While these two promises offer divine assurance, there is another one that predates them; God instructed Moses to tell Aaron and his sons how to bless the children of Israel (Numbers 6:23). That promise of blessing is often used as a benediction but has implications that extend beyond the end of a service. Accordingly, it will be used to day to anchor our sermon entitled *Divine Protection*.

To proper anchor the sermon, the attention is focused on a brief background on the textual base. It was lifted from the book of Numbers—not the type that some people play. This book instead, was one of the five that Moses wrote. In terms of history, Numbers is the account the forty years of wandering in the wilderness. It highlights God's jobs for Moses and Aaron on the journey. Moses, God chose as leader and Aaron—Moses' brother—as the priest. Moses was responsible for the overall leadership of the Israelites while Aaron oversaw their spiritual activities.

In the text of this sermon, God instructed Moses to have Aaron utter a blessing of protection on the Israelites. That prayer is found in Numbers 6:22–27. As noted therein, it assured the Israelites of triune blessing—that is from God, Jesus, and the building of a hedge around Job.

Beloved, in addition to providing protection for us, the Lord is willing and able to shower us with happiness, tranquility, and peace. Aaron was fully aware of this divine desire and capacity as found in the words. The Lord makes his face shine upon you. With this divine provision, we become soaked up in light, joy, contentment, and zest for living. These and numerous other divine privileges are ours for the prayerful asking, but the somber question—our last consideration—becomes have we decided to let God be God, to invite the Holy Spirit into our life, and to follow the teaching of Micah—love mercy, do justly, and walk humble with thy God (6:8). Beloved, the Lord loves us and stands ever ready to help us if we would just allow God to be God.

In closing, a personal question is posed for all there assembled. "Do you feel the need for divine protection as you move along the pathway of life?" If not, continue the broad road that leads to destruction. In contrast, should you feel the need for divine protection. Prayerfully call upon the Lord "to bless you and keep you, to make his face shine upon you, and be gracious unto you, to lift up his countenance upon you and give you peace." Amen!

Holy Spirit

Against this background on the text, let us now turn to the earlier specified topics contained in the subject, the first of which is the three-fold basis of divine protections. As noted in the text, the word *Lord* is used three different times; first, the Lord bless thee; next, the Lord make his face upon thee; and third, the Lord lift his countenance upon thee. Notice, this Aaronic utterance mentioned the Lord three times—a signal of the triune God. In brief, it tells us that God blesses us, Jesus shines upon us, and the Holy Spirit lifts us up.

With this glorious assurance, let us turn to the second aspect of the subject, which is the Lord blesses us according to our needs. It is an unfortunate fact that too many of us have limited knowledge of our essential needs. We are too prone to being influenced by advertisement, our neighbors, of coworkers, and even our selfish motives. What is needed to offset this egoistic view of needs is a return to this prayer of Moses. In doing so, we will find that the Lord will bless us with health, prosperity, and peace of mind. In doing so, we will find that the Lord will protect us from hurt, harm, and danger. Satan was even aware of this divine protection when he accused God.

CHAPTER 12

SELECTIVE DIMENSIONS OF THE LIFE CYCLE

Selective Dimensions of the Life Cycle

A. The "Personality" or Total Person

    1.   Innate characteristics: gender, race, eye color, I.Q. ...
    2.   Original cultures: geography, family, language
    3.   Unique experiences: events known on to the person

B. Basic Needs

    1.   Food: baby, childhood, junk food, regular foods
    2.   Clothing: baby wear, adolescent styles, adult, work
    3.   Shelter: home, college, apartment, personal house

C. Socialization

    1.   Informal: acculturation, family, playgroups, relatives
    2.   Formal: school mates, college peers, workforce
    3.   Specialized: occupational training: pilot, investigator

D. Economic Resources

1. Informal: family, charities, soliciting
2. Formal: contractual, retirement, investment, SS, SSI

E. Adult Living Arrangements

1. Independent: personal apartment, house, others
2. Quasi-independent: residing in echo house, mobile home
3. Assisted Living: a facility that offers residence, food, care
4. Personal Care Home: a facility that offers residence, care assistant

F. Nursing Home: maximum services: residence, food, bed care

G. Essential Planning

1. The Living Will: stipulation of use of body as donor or not
2. Medical Directive: authorizing one to make medical decisions
3. Economic: Trust, deeds, will, administrator
    a. Establishing funds for family, church, or other charities
    b. Conveying title to properties and other assets
    c. Outlining how one plans possessions to be distributed
    d. Person legally authorized to probate will and/or Estate

H. Funeral plans and expenses

1. Preneed arrangements
2. Prepare program for eulogistic services

CHAPTER 13

ENDING TO THE BEGINNING

I am Alpha and Omega, the beginning and the end.
—Revelations 21:6

The book of Revelation is associated with the end of life and its aftermath. So to select a sermon anchor for the first Sunday of the year 2021 may well cause ambivalence regarding its application to the new calendar year.

In the book of Revelation, John records that Jesus said of himself, "I am Alpha and Omega, the beginning and the ending." That assertion shows that Jesus is infinite whereas humankind is finite. Jesus is immune to time whereas the humanity is intricately woven into time. Accordingly, the human group must think and live within a time boundary. Accordingly, humanity functions with a time established *box* known as the calendar.

The sermon topic for today was selected to explore some implications of time in human existence. It was entitled *The End and the Beginning*. The sermon will be undergirded by the following dimensions, namely: Response to the calendar's end of the year, response to the mortal end of life, and your response these ends.

Since the textual anchor was lifted from the book of Revelation, the most symbolic book of the Bible, it is deemed appropriate to provide some background information on this book. Its author is Saint John, who was exiled to the island of Patmos. The book was written between AD 05/96. It is referred to as the Revelation of Saint John the Divine. It "can only be properly understood in the light of scores of symbols." The book is an apocalypse, or view of events yet to come.

His apocalypse was multifaceted. It included a new heaven and a new Earth, the great white throne judgment, and the end of time. The date of this finality was not revealed to him, but John was fully convinced that this would even occur in accordance with God's plan. With these sketchy observations of Revelation, attention will now be focused on the earlier specified three concerns of the sermon, the first of which is response to the calendar's end of the year. Twenty-twenty has come to an end. That event usually encompassed innumerable activities.

Humanity must now turn to the Bible for teachings on the change from ending to beginning. The sermon, in this connection, will submit a few biblical teachings on the change. The Holy Bible is replete with references to the inevitability of death.

The references are found in both testaments, and they include assertions about death, designation of persons who died, statements on the certainty of death, names of persons who died, the unknown time of death, and the reward after death for having been faithful in mortal life.

The Bible, among its many topics, can be studied as a chronology of decedents—persons who lived and died. Symbolically, their life, like 2021, had an ending and their immortality, like 2021, was the new beginning. Beloved, all of us, along with the whole of humanity, will ultimately encounter the same reality. In support of this somber event, attention will now be directed to a few scriptural citations. The list is by no means exhaustive. It is rather a partial delineation. It includes, "A time to be born and a time to die" (Ecclesiastes 3:2), "Is there not an appointed time to man upon the earth" (Job 7:1), "Man that is born of woman is of few days and full of trouble" (Job 14:1), "Yea, though I walk through the valley of the shadow, I will fear no evil" (Psalm 23:4), "And the day of death than the day of birth" (Ecclesiastes 7:1), "Man goeth to this long home, and his mourners go about the street" (Ecclesiastes 12:7), "Watch therefore: For ye know not what hour your Lord doth come" (Matthew 24:42), "If we have been planted—died—in his likeness, we shall be also in the likeness of his resurrection" (Romans 6:5), "And in those days shall men seek death, and shall desire to die, and death shall flee from them" (Revelation 9:6), "Be thou faithful unto death, and I will give thee a life" (Revelations 2:10).

Beloved, let us take confidence in the power of Jesus to deliver on his promise. Remember, he said himself, "I am Alpha and Omega, the beginning and the end, the first and the last" (Revelations 22:13). This glorious assurance leads to the third phase of the sermon which is—What is your response to the ending and beginning phenomenon of life? As noted in the sermon, there are two crucial areas that humanity face; they are the calendar time frame, and the life sojourn. The first is general knowledge and earthly experiences for humankind. Each normal person knows and experiences the passing of the Old Year and the entrance of the New Year.

The second area, however, is encumbered by a common reality for everyone. That problem is the fact that, while knowing about the beginning of life, one has never experienced the ending of life nor its consequences. Hence, there is an urgent need. First, for information about and making plans for the end of physical life, and secondly, being or becoming firmly committed to Jesus as Lord and Savior. It is in response to the second need—that of passing from life to death—that this final phase of the sermon is directed. Unlike the physician or attorney who used their training and professional references, this pastor is using his training and professional book—the Holy Bible—to present the prescription for the ending of life and preparation for the immortal existence.

Heading the list of spiritual medication is the fact that there is a time to be born and a time to die. This certainty leads to a daily dose of prayer and thanksgiving. Remember the Bible teaches that man ought to always pray. Another ingredient of the spiritual medication includes regular exercise in helping the needy as described in Matthew (25:31–46). Remain confident in the Lord to walk with you through the valley of the shadow of death, and before retiring at night think of, if not utter, the childhood prayer. Now lay me down to sleep, I pray the Lord my soul to keep, if I should die before I wake, I pray the Lord my soul to take. Amen.

CHAPTER 14

THE BIBLE: NATURE
AND VALUE

If there ever was a time we need the Bible, it's now.
—EGSJ 1.9.22

"All scripture is given by the inspiration of God, and it is profitable for doctrine, for reproof, for correction, for instruction in righteousness" (2 Timothy 3:16). There are many different religions in the world. Most of them have their sacred book(s) in which are found history, the founder(s), beliefs, expectations, and outcomes at the end of life. Those sacred books are known by a conventionalized name endemic to a specific religion. In Christianity, for example, the sacred book is known as the Bible. Without attempting to critique the sacred books of the religions, the sermon today will be confined to the Bible as the sacred book for the religion of Christianity.

The sermon will encompass the following divisions, which are highlights on the Bible, the authenticity of the Bible, and values of the Bible as taught by Saint Paul. It is undergirded by the intent of providing a deeper understanding of and appreciation for the

Bible, the book that President George Washington described as "the best gift God has ever given to man. All of the good from the Savior of the world is communicated to us through this book." Against this Washingtonian assertion, attention will be directed to the earlier specified objectives, the first of which is the selective highlights of the Bible. The word Bible comes from the Latin word *biblia,* which means a paper(s) or scroll. It is an ancient collection of writings, comprised of sixty-six separate books, written over approximately 1600, by at least forty distinct authors.

The Bible is divided into two divisions which are The Old Testament with thirty-nine books and the New Testaments with twenty-seven books. The two divisions can be contrasted. Thusly, the Old Testament is prophecy while the new is fulfillment; the Old Testament is law while the New Testament is grace. The Old Testament describes the beginning of everything and the New Testament describes the ending of everything.

The Protestant Bible encompasses sixty-six books while omitting the twelve books known as the Apocrypha; these books are included in the Catholic Bible but were excluded in the canonization process.

The Bible has a lengthy history of revisions and/or writers. A few of the widely recognized ones are the American Standard Version, the Holman Study Bible, the New International Version, the Chronological Study Bible, the Catholic Bible, and the King James Version (KJV) of 1611. While recognizing the significance of these and other translations of the Bible, the position here at Institutional First Baptist Church is anchored in the King James Version because it is traced back to Antioch, the place where believers were first called Christians.

Irrespective of the translations, all the translations concur that the Bible is the Word of God. This divine certainty leads to the second dimension of the sermon which is the authenticity of the Bible. Unlike academic thesis, dissertation, research papers, editorial, novels, and textbooks, all being the product of human thought and/or research, the Bible was divinely inspired. Support for this fact was set forth by Peter who wrote, "Knowing this first, that no prophesy of scripture is of any private interpretation. For the prophecy came not in old time by the will of man. But holy men of God spoke as they were moved by the Holy Spirit" (2 Peter 1:20–21). The apostle Paul's writings also documented the authentic base of the Bible. He averred that "All scripture is given by inspiration of God..." (2 Timothy 3: 16). These two citations regarding the Bible as the Word of God, certify that the Bible is inerrant in message and eternal in longevity. This glorious message leads to the final consideration of the sermon which is the values of the Bible for Christian living. Prior to specifying some values, attention is called to some of its universal teachings on life in general. The Bible asserts that humankind was created by God. Initially, it lived in a state of peace with God. Soon, it committed a transgression against God. It was expelled from the Garden of Eden. It became known as a sinner by nature. It was offered redemption though the sacrificial blood of Jesus and it is charged to be faithful unto death and thereby gain access to eternal life.

There are innumerable teachings, precepts, and mandates for pursuance in Christian living. However, the sermon will be confined to those found in the text as recorded by Paul in his second letter to Timothy. Therein, he reminded him that the "Scripture is given by the inspiration of God," and immediately preceded to specify values of the Scripture in Christian living. First, Paul stated that Scripture is profitable for doctrine involving biblical truths and human formulation of beliefs and actions. It is an unfortunate fact that many individuals and/or groups have neglected and/or distorted the Scripture in developing their religious beliefs; such groups are known in theology as cults. Paul, secondly, indicated that Scripture is profitable for reproof; this word, reproof, denoted the pattern of action to follow when experiencing criticism for an action or a fault. Essentially, it calls for mildness and prayer as noted in Psalm 37:1–2 "Fret not thyself because of evil doers, neither be thou envious against worker of iniquity." Regarding such devious individuals, the Scripture teaches that they shall soon be cut down like the grass, and wither as the green herb.

While recognizing that injustices are often imposed by others, he was, at the same time, aware of the fact that human nature can lure an individual into transgress. He recorded the account of his dilemma in Romans 7:19 where he wrote, "For the good that I would I do not: but the evil which I would not, that I do." But using the Scripture, he gave thanks unto God who would deliver him for the body of death. Using that personal experience, Paul told Timothy that the Scripture is profitable for use in seeking correction for erroneous behaviors. To reduce, if not to eliminate, the need for correction, it is recommended that the believer would concur with the Psalmist's commitment, "I have hidden thy word in my heart that I might not sin against God."

The fourth and final value of the Scripture in the sermon is its instruction in righteousness. As used herein, this word refers to living a life aligned with Scriptural teachings. Such a lifestyle includes faith, prayer, benevolence, patience, and looking unto Him who is the author and finisher of one's faith.

In closing, let us remember the adage—the race is not to the swift nor strong, but to the one who can endure to the end. Remember! The Bible is the Word of God. Jesus is the Son of God. The Holy Spirit is the Comforter from God. The Gospel is the good news of God's Salvation. Prayer is the channel through which petitions reach the heart of God, and Faith is the essence of hoping for things unseen. Amen.

This brief statement undergirds the biblical anchor of this study entitled *Beyond the Fear of Death.*

EPILOGUE

AUTHOR/BOOK

This book is an eclectic study of some dimensions of learning about the reality of living, but ultimately dying. This book, although written by a person with multiple academic credential degrees, teaching areas, and anchored by the Jude Christian Religion is no attempt to make or convert believers into Christianity even though this author also holds graduate degrees in religion but makes no attempt to impose his faith upon people including members of the church where he serves as pastor.

This book is a valuable resource for reading various dimensions on health, motivation to seek professional services, along with prayer and reading from the Bible (KJV). Additionally, this book strongly recommends seeking guidance from doctors with professional training around the reader's concern. As a closing thought, please observe the following warnings:

1. 1.   Seek medical advice and treatment.
2. 2.   Do not consume medicine prescribed for another person.
3. 3.   Avoid the so-called home remedies.

4. 4.   Avoid trying to get a little shot of whiskey.
5. 5.   I strongly recommend reading your Bible.
6. 6.   <u>Lastly, human life is about a short transition between birth and death.</u>

The Author,

EG Sherman, Jr., PhD, DST, DA, DD, DHL
Thank you, Mrs. Phyllis Plummer, my typist.

Sources
The author's library
The King James Version of the Bible (KJV)

Special addition for Epilogue—page 69—Although this book on prayer was released on 2017 and prayer was effective then and continues to be effective now (2021). It must be noted that many of the social, political, and demographic changes—all exert some impact on human views of prayer. Accordingly, a few observations will be noted in this epilogue.

In addition to the original epilogue, it is noted the current one must acknowledge, not to change prayer but to identify current distractions to some prayers.

This document is an eclectic study of some dimensions of death and dying. It is designed to provide some comfort for persons in the death and dying reality. No medical recommendations are herein submitted. Instead, this book seeks to provide comfort and hope for person coping with death and dying. Hopefully, the person of reference can hold in its hands a Bible, or listen to a benevolent person, or hear a kind person read. Remember, Doc said, "Life is but a transition between birth and death."

ABOUT THE AUTHOR

EG Sherman, Jr., PhD, holds three doctorate degrees. He is a professor emeritus of sociology, history, philosophy, along with credentials in gerontology and microcomputer from Albany State University, Albany, Georgia. He is also a retired vice president for academic affairs at Bethany Divinity College and Seminary in Dothan, Alabama, founding pastor of the Institutional First Baptist Church, Albany, Georgia, owns the website www.biblicalechoes02.com, and has authored four religiously anchored books. He has been widowed since the passing of his wife of thirty-nine years; they had no children.

He retired as in educator in 2002; professor, administrator, consultant. Following retirement turned to a latent desire, writing. In pursuit of desired, he published five books and over halfway on number six. As a certified theologian, his focus is theological/heavy social implications. He has held several books signing but dislike the traveling and net profit. Hence, he is seeking a marketing company for all five of his books and future ones. A complete list of his publications can be found on: amazon.com/author/eugenesherman/. You can also contact him through: 229-430-0066. His weekly sermons can be viewed on Biblicalechoes02.